LOVE IS ALL THERE IS

Remembering Your True Self

◆

Daryl Chang

Front cover image: pixabay.com – Alexey Hulsov [Alexey_Hulsov].
Inside images: pixabay.com – Gordon Johnson [GDJ], Alexandra Koch
                   [Alexandra_Koch], Clker-Free-Vector-Images, MJ Jin
                   [La_Petite_Femme], msyanasoo, Rosy [RosZie], Phuong Thai Thi
                   Quynh [PhuongLucky], Natalia Aggiato [nat aggiato].

LOVE IS ALL THERE IS: Remembering Your True Self
Daryl Chang
ISBN-13: 978-1-7389410-4-9

Personal Growth, Body Mind & Spirit, Self-help, Spirituality

Also by Daryl Chang
MASQUERADE: The Life Game God Plays
THE MIND OF GOD: Life Behind The Scenes
HEAVEN "ARE WE THERE YET?" A Guide To Your Way Back Home

*The way to heal the world is not by seeking to change
what is on the outside but by first changing what is on the inside.*

It begins with you.

Know thyself.
You are an extraordinary being.

*You are a unique expression of Love
who is created from an infinite source of Love
and is here to extend this Love.*

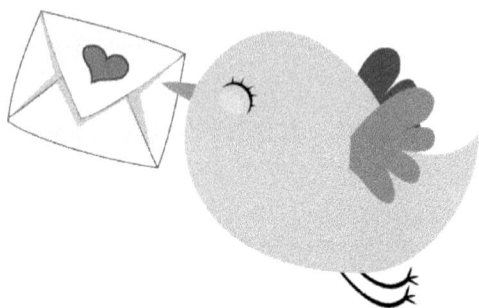

LOVE
IS ALL THERE IS

CONTENTS

♦

Author's Note

♦

When I look upon this world, there are considerable man-made theories, suggestions, dogma, and superstitions. I see people who are distracted, busy, overwhelmed, exhausted, and carrying on in a robotic way never really questioning the world they are living in but accepting it as normal. I have thought that there is something much more to life than what the world seems to operate on. I know something is not right and for the longest time I could not put my finger on it.

This world where hatred, war and violence, intentional destruction of the planet, poverty, dis-ease, anger, fear, cruelty, greed, envy, et cetera exists is nonsensical to me. This world feels unnatural to me. This world is insane to me.

What feels more natural to me are the feelings of love, joy, happiness, peace, sharing, caring, compassion, et cetera. I have always genuinely wanted to understand and know this thing called Love, how it heals all things and is the answer to all things. As such, I voraciously read books and gravitated to teachings about these things, trying to figure out how to apply it in my own life.

I have observed, contemplated, and gained greater clarity. I have read many great books so far. I am deeply grateful to all the souls who have taken and do take the time to share and communicate the Truth in the written word. All books express in its own way, one Truth. I complete one, feel like it is the last book I need to read, but then another comes into my awareness that is even more affirming for me. As time progresses, I move further beyond a mere intellectual understanding of Love to a greater embodiment of it. I recognize that such experiences never end because I am forever learning about my Self and each encounter is a stepping stone to guide me home to the presence of Love.

I learn what I want to teach and I teach what I want to learn so that I may learn more deeply of my Self. To teach is to demonstrate and to demonstrate is to teach. "Love Is All There Is" is based on what I have learnt through the many years and many teachings I have gained.

The Truth is simple. I write this book as simply as I can in my own personal expression to not only help you understand this thing we call Love but to inspire you to practice and apply it yourself. I do this not because someone is requiring or paying me to do it. It arises within the field of the Mind of God that is the essence of all that I am, as you are. I witness and allow it to come through me so that the work is done and thusly extend the Love. I write this book for you, one reader at a time if necessary, with the intention to help all remember to be the Love they are so the Kingdom of God that is wholly Love is restored rightfully.

May you be transformed by the journey of remembering who you are.

With love and gratitude,

Daryl

Preface

◆

Take away all of fear and its derivatives (ie. evil, hatred, greed, envy, et cetera), what do you have? Love. Love is all that remains.

Take away all that is false, all that are lies, what do you have? Truth. Truth is all that remains.

Take away all that is illusion, what do you have? Reality. Reality is all that remains.

Take away all that is not good, what do you have? Good. Good is all that remains.

Take away all of your physical self, what do you have? Spirit. Spirit is all that remains.

Take away all of the world, what do you have? Nothing. Everything. God is all that remains.

Take away all that is not you, what do you have? You. You and your divinity are all that remains. You are Love, Truth, Reality, Good, Spirit, God. You are perfection.

If you truly wish for a beautiful life and a beautiful world, you must recognize, know, accept, and be(come) who and what you were created to be and are.

Love gives you a sense of conquering all;
that everything is possible and nothing impossible.

Prologue

♦

According to an old Hindu legend, there was a time long ago when all beings on Earth were gods but they started to wrongly use their divinity.

Thusly, Brahma (the Creator) decided to take away divinity from all beings and to hide it somewhere they could never find it. Brahma called a council of gods to help him decide of a place to hide this divinity.

Some suggested, "Let's bury it deep inside the earth." To this, Brahma answered, "No, humans will dig deep into the earth and find it."

Some god suggested, "Let's sink it deep into the ocean." Again Brahma said, "No, humans will learn to dive deep into the ocean and find it."

After thinking a while, some suggested, "Let's hide it at the top of a mountain." Again Brahma replied, "No, humans will eventually climb up the highest mountain and take up their divinity."

Then all gods gave up and said, "It seems like there is no place on Earth to hide divinity where human beings will eventually not reach."

Brahma thought for a long time and said, "We will hide their divinity deep into the centre of their own being. Humans will search for it here and there but they will not look for divinity inside their true self."

All gods agreed this was the best place for hiding divinity and the deed was done. Since then, humans have been going up and down, digging, climbing, diving, exploring, and searching for something —God— which lies within themselves.

This book aspires to show you that this legend is neither a complete myth nor story; that you are God (still); that your divinity is stored within you; that you abuse, misuse, or are ignorant of your divinity; that you have not sought your divinity but should you consciously seek it, you will find it; that you have forgotten your divinity but should you remember, you can begin to rightly use it again.

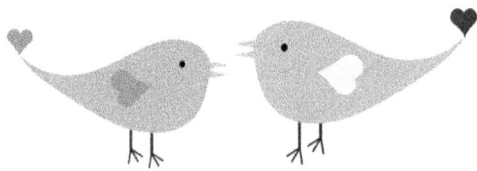

Love is the only thing worth valuing.

Introduction

♦

You have been mired in this false world forever and oblivious to your divinity. You have strayed far away from the wholly Love you are, deprived yourself of eternal joy, made yourself a prisoner of your own device, and are presently living the falsehood of an impostor.

Recognition of your divinity is foundational to you experiencing a life filled with joy, peace, and happiness. Do not overly concern yourself if you are unfamiliar with this yet. If you are open to this apparently simple declaration, then you can contribute to a joyous world and to your own joyous life. The realization of this Truth will come over time when you decide to nurture the knowledge you gain about your divinity.

You, my dear friend who has begun to read this book, let us say you do not presently understand your existence and your divinity. How would you prefer someone who wishes to reveal the beauty and significance of divinity in your life, to initiate a conversation with you about it? What would make you be open, welcome, and embrace such a dialogue from another?

Conversely, imagine for a moment you presently understand your existence and your divinity. How would you initiate a conversation about divinity with another who knows nothing of it and has never thought about it? How would you explain what divinity is and where it lies? How would you convey the significance of divinity in one's life?

Let us say that you are such one and I the other and we have found a way to at least start such a conversation. What a grand and glorious step that is.

When you are resistant to thoughts and ideas that are contrary to your beliefs, I encourage you to ask yourself, "Why am I unwilling to believe the possibility of this Truth? Why do I believe this to be untrue and what I presently believe to be true? Is what I currently believe, something I have proved or is it something handed to me by race, superstition, suggestion, or man-made theories?"

Read with an open mind that enjoys freedom from belief and judgment. Read also with an open heart. For the heart is that which feels, allows, embraces, and trusts things. The heart is that which guides you home to Love. It is only by taking risks, by opening ourselves to new ideas, to new ways of looking at ourselves and at life, that we learn, grow, expand, become better, and become who we really are.

Growth, development, and evolution of yourself is impeded when your mind is closed; when you stay stubborn to your beliefs thinking what you know is absolute; when you immediately reject any sincere discussion dissimilar to your beliefs. Put aside your preconceived notions, your psychological defense mechanisms, and your prejudices. Take a chance on remembering that new information could well grant you complete spiritual freedom. Let us not get too far ahead of ourselves but begin first a pleasant conversation.

This world you seem to live in is not home to you. Somewhere in your heart and mind, you know that this is true. What you know you cannot explain but you feel it. I have felt it my entire life, that there is something wrong with this world. I feel outside here, from somewhere all unknown. Just a persistent feeling, sometimes not more than a tiny throb, at other times hardly remembered, actively dismissed, but surely to return to my mind again.

The world has been pulled over your eyes to blind you from the Truth. You are a slave in this false world. You were born into bondage. You were born into a prison —a prison for your mind—. You are a prisoner here of your own device. Free your mind.

You have to let it all go —fear, doubt, guilt, belief, judgment, limitation, unworthiness—. Let it go without delay like the rope that is scorching your hands in a fun tug-of-war game for it no longer serves you. Your true Self knows no fear, nor can conceive of loss or suffering or death. When there is an absence of fear, which means that you are filled with Love only, there is a presence of conquering. Peace is the result when one has conquered his greatest fears and is consumed by Love only.

When you come into this world, you automatically begin participating in social consciousness without ever having explicitly consented to it. In actuality, you are by default, sovereign. That is, you are free, self-governing, loving, supreme, autonomous, and independent.

Daryl Chang

When you come into this world, you follow the lead of your parents, who got their lead from their parents and society. If your parents have been accustomed to the reality handed them based on deceit, then they in turn pass down this reality to you. If you continue to follow the reality of social consciousness without ever questioning the validity of it, then you too will live as they do. By never reflecting, you will not know of the falsity of your current existence; of your divinity and your inheritance; of your rightful heirship which has been withheld from you.

Your soul urges you to learn the Truth that has been lost; to become the Divine principle you have forgotten long ago. It is most important that you learn of your own divinity as well as everyone else's. I write this book in my own personal expression to help you gain clarity of your divinity and its relation to the universe.

All the love, wisdom, and power to you.

Love is your innate natural state;
fear is a learned unnatural state.

PART
ONE

The Awakening

♦

ONE

There is an old story of a scholar and a Zen master. The scholar had an extensive background in Buddhist studies. He wanted to study with the master and asked him to teach him Zen. He began to talk about his extensive doctrinal background and went on and on about the many treatises and philosophies he had studied. The master listened patiently for a while and then began to brew a pot of tea. When the tea was ready, the master poured it into the scholar's cup. He kept pouring until the tea began to overflow and run all over the floor. The scholar saw what was happening and shouted, "Stop, stop! The cup is full. You can't get any more in!" The master stopped pouring and said, "You are like this cup. You are full of ideas about Buddha's Way. You come to me and ask for teaching but your cup is full. I can't put anything more in. Before I can teach you, you'll have to empty your cup."

You might be that scholarly squirrel who has gathered lots of nuts of man-made theories, superstitions, dogma, beliefs, and suggestions, and filled your nut-cup, that is your mind, so full that you really are not able and willing to learn more about God, Love, and Life, even if it is Truth.

If you have picked up this book to read, then bravo, maybe your cup is not entirely full yet. Nonetheless, I would still encourage you to empty your cup. That is, become as a child again where you are pure, innocent, and know nothing. Why? The thoughts herein will be a complete reversal of your current thinking. The thoughts will require you to "see" beyond your physical eyes and from a different perspective; to observe yourself rather than observe the world. They may seem wholly insane because you have been living in this world for quite some time now from a certain perspective. Insanity seems sane to those who are insane, and sanity seems insane to those who are insane. That is how it is. It will be like you wearing your t-shirt inside out and not knowing till someone tells you. Allow yourself to see things differently what you insist must be seen in a certain way. Start anew.

Daryl Chang

At this very moment, you may openly admit to yourself that you are not free. In fact, you may concede that each day you feel less and less free. You feel tied down or shackled in this world.

If you are genuinely sick and tired of any or all of the nonsense in this world and have the slightest iota of desire that this world be of Love only, then I trust you will continue reading. You, like every human being, are capable of so much more than where you are. So at this moment, your first willing commitment should be like, "Yes, I do want a world full of Love only. I will read with an open mind and heart." Do not fret. This is not a marriage proposal. This is just a commitment to yourself only and you are free to break it whenever without any guilt.

You are busy but take your time. You are not going to be scolded or put in detention but you cannot be lackadaisical with this Love thing. Check in with yourself periodically when you are not making sense of something and ask, "Did I read with only half my focus because I was watching the hockey game or that action flick, trying to get dinner ready, or playing with the kids?" You may realize that you missed something and need to read it again. Just go back and really set some quiet time in which you deliberately put the world aside and focus.

Before you and I get going, there is something important that I would like you to recognize. That something is words.

Words are of great consequence because they are powerful. They can be used like weapons, wielded in Love or fear. In general, words are not intentionally used as weapons, and should not be, but as a means to communicate and express thoughts with one another. Words are one of many human forms and are merely symbols of symbols.

From an intellectual standpoint, words are deemed important and necessary to identify and describe the things in this world we live in. In reality, each and every thing in the world exists in spite of the words we use to do as such. For instance, the sun shines even without being called the sun, a tree grows even without being called a tree, and water nourishes even without being called water.

Words by its own nature ironically pose a hazard in its very purpose of communication and expression. Words require the understanding of other words to understand the meaning of the word itself. Your interpretation or understanding of a word's meaning is influenced by your past thoughts and beliefs. Feelings such as conflict, frustration, or annoyance may arise between two persons when they are not synchronized in the meaning of a word.

Communication between two minds requires only the willingness to join in communion. Communion requires the willingness to retract one's investment in being right. Both minds recognize and concede that each does not really know what a single thing in this world is for.

Understanding Love will be an incremental task. By this I mean that words and ideas are stepping stones to the Truth of Love. If you do not fully understand the meaning of a word or an idea, you may potentially have difficulty making progress to the ultimate you seek —*Love*—.

There is another important thing that I would like you to recognize. That something is circular references. A circular reference is such that a word is used to reference the meaning of another word and vice versa. This occurs since all words ultimately are defined in terms of other words. Many things, if not all, will be a paradox. For practical purposes, what this means is simply that you may need to read through the whole of the book to appreciate each part and the sum of the parts.

One of the first things to establish in your journey to understanding Love is God. For the only relationship that holds any value at all is your relationship with God, your creative Source.

This world has successfully defamed God to create numerous factions: atheists who do not believe in God; agnostics who do not know what to believe of God; and firm believers who believe in God outside of themselves and a God of man's societal making.

This world has successfully turned many away from God through endless atrocities such as war, poverty, and dis-ease. There are individuals who have had dreadful experiences brought up in religious families and view God with absolute disdain. As such, many have closed their mind to God.

If you are such an individual finding yourself hesitant to continue here, you need to be willing to overcome your aversion to this word. You must temporarily suspend judgment and defense of your beliefs and feelings. You must be open to the possibility that what you have been manipulated to believe or not believe is untrue.

Daryl Chang

Now, we begin by making our first declaration.

— You and God are one. —

The aforementioned is a profound declaration from where you believe yourself to be. That is, you believe you are separate from God. To take an initial leap of faith in it, you will need to make time to contemplate.

Put a seed into the soil. In a relatively short time, it sprouts, breaks the surface, and grows. Ask yourself, "How does it do this?" Did it go to a plant school during the time it was underground to earn a degree to learn how to do this? Really, how does it know how to do this? There must be a higher power, a higher intelligence that is doing this.

Observe a bird flying in the sky. Ask yourself, "How does it do this?" Does it go to some bird aviation school to earn a degree to learn how to do this? Really, how does it know how to do this? There must be a higher power, a higher intelligence that is doing this.

Contemplate anything in nature and ask the same question. You will end up with the same answer.

Reflect on a mother having a baby. At no time does the mother personally provide instructions to the things inside her body to do this and do that to grow the baby. The baby just develops. Just like the seed, ask yourself, "How does it do this?" There is a higher power, a higher intelligence that is doing this.

Now, turn to yourself. Contemplate on your breathing. Do you "do" 'breathing'? That is, do you personally instruct yourself, your body, on how to go about breathing? You do not. It just happens. Do you "do" 'circulating blood'? Do you personally instruct your body on how to circulate your blood and distribute the oxygen throughout? You do not. It just happens. Do you "do" 'digesting food'? Do you personally instruct your body and coordinate all your organs to digest your food? You do not. It just happens. So if you are not doing the breathing, the blood circulating, and the food digesting, then who is doing it? I will give you a clue. It is not Peter, Paul, or Mary. Did you answer the question yourself? It is the higher power, the higher intelligence. It is God. God is in you, just as It is in me, the seed, the flower, the tree, the bird, the squirrel, the sun, the moon, the air, and so on and so on. It is in everything. God is in all. God is all in all.

The aforesaid statement may be unfathomable and not so easy to accept as true presently. But this is just a habit from your limited intellectual thinking because you are not conscious of who you are yet. This is the irony of your current predicament —a predicament that is the foundation to the apparent problems and solution of this world—. It is not arrogance to think you are God when you are. It is ignorance to think you are not when you are. You need only to recognize, know, and accept this Truth.

Proclaiming you and God are one, or more simply, you are God, is not difficult as you may make it out to be. You do not do so by means of blind faith for that is unnecessary. You accept it as fact, a Truth. You accept it with the same knowing as when someone asks you your name. It is what it is and who you know yourself to be.

If you have remained open at this point, then this Truth is now a seed in your consciousness. If you nurture this seed by providing it with proper soil, water, and sun, then the Truth of yourself will be revealed in time and you will live up to your full potential. The question right now is, "Are you willing to nurture this seed to an expanded awareness of who you are and what is possible for you in life, one that is filled with joy?"

Freedom is Love under all conditions. That is, to be free means to be Love always. Until you genuinely understand Love and the Truth of who you are, you will never be free. Hence if you indeed wish to be free, set aside time to withdraw yourself from the busyness, roar, and din of the world. Have the willingness to take the time to learn, to remember, and to know that God dwells in you and is you.

Now, we begin to establish who or what God is.

God is the Source of all creation.

God is omnipotent, omnipresent, and omniscient. That is, It is all-powerful, all-around, and all-knowing.

God is the formless invisible animating intelligent force of energy — *pure unlimited Spirit*— that penetrates, permeates, and fills the spaces and interspaces of the universe of which it is Itself. God is also the visible forms produced from its invisible Self. God is the sum of all things visible and invisible. That is, God is all in all.

Daryl Chang

God is eternal and infinite. God has no beginning and no end. God is perpetually expanding. God is your supply and It is infinite or inexhaustible.

God is consciousness. It is the Universal Mind, the One Mind. It is the Supreme or Infinite Intelligence.

God is absolute, whole, complete, and perfect.

God is wholly perfect good. God is merely a different way of spelling good. Contained within the word good is God and contained within God is good.

God is Truth. God is reality.

At this stage, we introduce Love and make a declaration.

— God is but Love and Love is the only reality. —

Love is commonly perceived in our society as merely an emotion. We say things such as we "love chocolate," we "love a good party," we "love our spouse," and on it goes —but we are referring to the emotion of feeling what we term love—. These forms are but mere physical expressions of a deeper spiritual love. You are unable yet to conceive of a Love devoid of or unattached to some personal interest.

Love in its ultimate form is God allowing the Life that It is to be an ongoingness through each of us.

Love is the allowance of all things. Love is the embrace of all things. Love is the trust in all things. That is, Love allows all things, embraces all things, trusts all things, and thereby transcends all things.

This is to say, Love gives all things complete freedom to be and do as they will. Love sets all things free.

From this, we can see easily then that Love is patient and kind; Love does not envy and does not boast; Love is not proud, is not rude, is not self-seeking, and is not easily angered. Love keeps no record of wrongs. Why? Because Love allows all things, embraces all things, trusts all things, and thereby transcends all things.

Love heals all things. How so? Because Love sets all things free. Love lets all things be and do as they will. Love sets things free again when they are not free.

So to love means to set things free, free to be what they want to be and free to do what they want to do; to release all things from judgment and perception; to desire joy, peace, happiness, and everything good for all things; to wish, confer, endow, favour, magnify, glorify, praise, or exalt all things divine (ie. abundance, prosperity, health, et cetera) upon a person, thing, place, event, situation, or experience; to see the Love and Light in all things; to satiate all things with the Love that is within you, that is you; to appreciate and bless with gratitude the creations before you for no reason other than it exists.

Love is a positive expansive vibrational energy. Love engenders all that is good such as joy, peace, love, and compassion. Love demonstrates itself in the likes of peace, abundance, health, freedom, and all things good.

What is not Love is fear. Fear is a negative contractive vibrational energy. Everything requires Love, even fear. For Love allows all things, embraces all things, trusts all things, and thereby transcends all things.

Fear casts a shadow on Love and has no effect except obstructing your recognition of Love. Fear constricts your creativity, your Love, your unlimitedness, your everything. Fear engenders all that is not good such as sorrow, hatred, anger, greed, envy, and all things unlike God. Fear demonstrates itself in the likes of war, poverty, dis-ease, bondage, and all things not good.

God, the Source of creation, is but Love. How so? Because God allows all things, embraces all things, trusts all things, and thereby transcends all things. This is reality, the only reality.

Creation never ceases; it is continuous, never-ending. If God was not Love, then the Life that God is would cease to exist in the next moment and it would never be again.

God is unlimited. God loves us so grandly that It allows everyone to create whatever they wish to create: the good and the evil, the positive and the negative, the pleasure and the pain.

Now, we progress to seeing more Truth and make a declaration.

— Whatever God is, you are. —

God is cause and you are effect.

You and God are one. You are as God created you to be. You are free. You are made in Its image and likeness. Know and accept that whatever God is, you are.

God is pure unlimited Spirit. You are pure unlimited spirit. You are not the body-mind.

God is the Source of creation. You are the source of your creations. You are a creator *always*. You are the creator, the creation process, and the creation itself.

God is consciousness. You are that consciousness who is aware of your Self and witnesses your creations.

God is omnipotent, omnipresent, and omniscient. That is, God is all-powerful, all-around, and all-knowing. You are Power and your own master. No one should ever wield power over you. You are all in all but you are unfamiliar with this as yet. You know the answer to all questions and all problems but you are presently not versed in this knowing.

God is absolute. You are absolute. The absolute cannot contain something within itself that is not itself. As there is no other, you must command yourself to be that which you claim to be or have. You dwell within every conception of yourself and from this inwardness. You transcend all conceptions of yourself only as you believe yourself to be that which you transcend.

God is whole and complete. You are whole and complete. You do not require anything or anyone to make you whole or complete as you already are. Again, you are unfamiliar with this as yet.

God is perfect. You are perfect but you are unfamiliar with this because of how you perceive perfection. You are the Power using the power to see yourself exactly as you are. Think gently of this statement.

God is wholly perfect good. You are wholly perfect good. Alas, you are unfamiliar with this as yet.

God is but Love. Therefore so are you. You are as God created you to be. You are wholly Love. You are a thought of Love in form. You are a unique expression of Love borne from an infinite source of Love. God lives through you. You are a child of God and are sent into this world to extend this Love. You are free, free to be and do as you will.

You are all of the aforementioned but you are presently not acting as such because you have forgotten it in this world. You may ask, "How did I forget this?" This answer is perhaps known by a few. You just have to accept that you have and begin the path of remembrance.

It is like when you lose your car key. You do not know how or why you lost it. You just know you want to find it. Or in many cases, you have been walking miles and hours everywhere. You completely forgot you even had a car and did not think to look for the car key to make getting around easier. But once you remember and find the key, you no longer tirelessly walk around.

You are reading this now and it is touching your soul. You are starting to remember what you have always known. There is now a slight crack in the clouds shrouding the sun that is God, and a ray of light from that Source that is you, is gradually shining through the darkness of the clouds that is this world.

Here now, we make another declaration that is important for you to remember always.

— Like begets like. —

Everything reproduces after its own kind. Like begets like. A chicken comes from a chicken not a duck. A salmon comes from a salmon not an oak tree. A squirrel comes from a squirrel not a human. Though each creature may have its own personality, the content or essence of it is the same. Imagine if you saw a horse waddle like a duck and quack like a duck, you would think the horse insane. The horse itself would not know it insane but you would. Imagine the new scene created if many horses around began to unknowingly mimic the insane horse because they themselves knew not what they were.

You are a child of God made of the same content and whose essence is Love but you are the horse who presently acts as a duck in this world because you have forgotten who and what you are. You see the other insane horses and accept that duck —*fear*— is just natural horse nature.

Remember henceforth always that everything reproduces after its own kind. Like begets like. Any thought, feeling, and action that is based on Love or fear will manifest in form respectively, for no other reason than to extend its own nature. That is, Love begets Love and fear begets fear. In the same way, peace begets peace; happiness begets happiness; joy begets joy; violence begets violence; hatred begets hatred; insanity begets insanity; and so on and so on. Hence, fear is dissolved only by extending Love. Love transforms fear. Love restores sanity, peace.

Children are extensions of their parents. They are forever connected to their parents. This is a bond that can never be broken. You are an extension of God. You are eternally connected to God. Just as you cannot shake your hand off your arm, you can never ever be separated.

You are a ray of light from the sun that is God. You are a drop of water from the ocean that is God. The content —*Love*— of you remains as your Source that is God.

Recall your commitment earlier that you desire a world full of Love only. Now, we expand on this commitment. You must decide to desire —above all things— to awaken to the perfect remembrance of your union with God; to think with the Mind of God. You are a sunbeam that finally decides to not be fearful of being a sunbeam and becomes aware of its infinite union with the sun itself. Be wholly committed to eliminating all that is unlike the Love of God in yourself. It will involve observing your own mind, your own behaviour, and your own reactions with the sense and softness of an innocent child. It will require you to cultivate deep self-honesty and ownership.

Now, we make a declaration.

— You create everything.
Nothing you experience is caused by anything outside of you. —

The first step to retrain the mind to become the Love you are is to acknowledge that you are a creator always of all that you perceive and to accept complete responsibility that you are creating everything.

Everything? Yes, everything. You create the pleasure, satisfaction, and ecstasy; you create the pain, disappointment, and suffering. You create the abundance, peace, and health; you create the lack, conflict, and illness. You originate everything. You are never the victim of anything. When you see yourself as a victim, you are erroneously choosing to use your God-given power to perceive yourself as being victimized.

The path to being the presence of Love begins when you accept total responsibility for the entire field of your experience. This includes the comings and goings of all beings, all encounters, and all deemed good and bad occurrences. There is nothing that you experience that is caused by anything outside of you. You experience only the effects of your own choice. Even when the world around you is not to your liking, you have to be humble, accept, and say, "I created this mess."

If you are even slightly resistant to this idea, it is because you have never really analyzed or scrutinized the things you create. If you bake a cake and it turns out "good", you will say, "I did that." But if the cake turns out "bad", you conveniently think of reasons like "It must have been the flour or the temperature of the oven." Maybe you plant a tomato seed. If it grows, you will say, "I did that." But if it fails to grow, you think, "It must have been a bad seed or not enough sunlight." Maybe you open a coffee shop and it is successful. You will say, "I did that." But if it fails, you think, "It must have been the location."

You never ventured to simply accept full responsibility that it is you who created the "bad" result. It takes great courage and self-honesty to look upon all your creations, however the result, with Love and the innocence of a child. To have your cake sink and flop, your garden wither and die, or your shop crash and burn, and yet smile and say, "I baked this cake, I planted this garden, I set up this shop. I and I alone have done this. Oh well. I will start over."

When you create something that is not up to snuff, you make several errors that affect your consciousness to stray from the Mind of God. You see and feel it as a failure. You see it and feel the cause of failure as outside of you rather than from within. The failure is not failure but a different experience to what you deem success. You create everything so the fault is but your own. You identify with the form of the failure; you see and feel that it is you; that it defines who you are. The failure is but a transient experience of what you falsely deem who you are.

Daryl Chang

By accepting full responsibility, recognizing you are creating everything, and observing what you are doing, you will discover that you are actually succeeding at it far more than you give yourself credit for. This insane world conditions you to put most of your energy into perceiving what is negative and failure and little into what is positive and success as God.

Never judge your creations or experiences especially when they are not to your liking. Rather, embrace them and feel gratitude for them. They are stepping stones to you growing into the Truth of who you are — Love—. See not the negativity but see the power you have in every moment and that nothing prevents you from choosing Love. For Love is not conditioned by the world. It is you —Love— that conditions the world. Look in awe of your power.

Learn to cultivate a deep enjoyment of whatever arises, seeing that all experiences are just reflections of your consciousness, and then adjust your thoughts if the forms are not to your liking.

Your mind has trained you to see the final form as the only thing you created. You do not think of all the in-between details as things you created but you have. Nothing comes to you unless you have called it from within yourself. The ingredients and oven you used to bake your cake, the tomato seed and plant stake you bought to grow your garden, and the building and customers you witness in your coffee shop, are all creations from the Mind of God that you brought into your awareness. You have indirectly created all but you have nonetheless created.

You think much of your daily life as ordinary but in each and every moment, extraordinary things are occurring. You must become aware that mundane things like brushing your teeth, drinking a glass of water, and sitting in a chair are all self-created. There is no level of difference —small or grand— between these and baking a cake, growing a garden, or opening a coffee shop. You created them all to have the experience of it. The fact that you exist confirms that you chose to create and experience. When you gain this true perspective and contemplate your actions, you will recognize it and say, "I have created. I have done this. And it is very good." Bring this to the forefront of your awareness. Own it. Realize that you are not here randomly just because you have to be. You are creating your experiences and your life.

You are a creator in every moment. You create physical things in this physical world but you also create qualities such as peace, compassion, and wisdom. It is a significant step to be conscious of your constant creation because you will begin to become aware of when your mind is thinking like God or unlike God. You will train your mind to think more rightly.

There is no perceived chaos, accident, or coincidence in the universe. Everything is orchestrated with elegant precision and unfaltering intelligence. Everything is an opportunity to learn about yourself. For each situation, circumstance, or experience, do not simply react with joy or disappointment but question it.

With all that surrounds you and the events, experiences, situations, and circumstances you encounter, particularly when it is not to your liking or someone is affecting you negatively, begin the habit of observing your own mind, your own behaviour, and your own reactions with a sense of wonder, innocence, and childlikeness. Be impersonal. Do not speak a word. Bring awareness to them. Ask yourself questions such as "Why did I bring this into my awareness? What is this trying to teach me about myself? What am I to learn? What do I truly believe about myself? What am I afraid of? What fear do I have that this is showing me? What aspect of me is this reflecting?"

When you move about throughout your day and feel the grass beneath your feet, know that you are the one using the power to create the body and to create the grass itself. You are the rain and the skin it falls upon. You are the sun, the moon, the flower, the puppy, the sound of laughter, and the smell of lavender. You are the creator, the creation process, and the creation itself. You are the one using the power to appreciate and to create the thing appreciated. You are the one using the power to smile and to create the thing that made you smile. You are the one using the power to frown and to create the thing that made you frown in disgust. You are the witness, the seer, the consciousness, the Self. You are everything. Having this perspective will serve you well.

When you know and accept you create everything —whether you deem it good or bad, positive or negative, liked or disliked— you will pause in your busyness and say, "Wow. I am good. I created. I did that." And you will smile. You will celebrate it. Then you will say, "I have called this to myself. Do I like and continue with it or do I dislike and choose something else?" You then continue creating as you desire.

Daryl Chang

Regardless of the creation and independent of the result, you know and understand the satisfaction that comes from creating. Freedom comes when you assume complete responsibility for the creation of your experiences, know who and what you are —Love—, and act in the Truth of it.

Here now, we make a very important declaration that is pivotal to your advancement to wholly understanding Love. It requires your astute attention and observation of its repercussions.

— You need nothing. —

"Need" is an expression of the perception that there is something you lack. Needing is quite different than wanting or choosing to do something. You can never be free if you feel you need. When you are free of need, you are free from being governed by the beliefs of this world, free to choose, and free to desire and create freely.

God needs nothing. Pure unlimited spirit needs nothing and seeks nothing. Pure unlimited spirit can only extend. Why? Because God is God. God is infinite. God is all in all. God has and is everything. You and God are one. You are as God created you to be. You have everything. As such, you need nothing and you need not seek anything. You seek nothing to acquire, accomplish, or resist. To feel the need of something or the need to do something is unnatural. There is never a moment when you lack anything at all. There is no need to fear. There is nothing to fear. Everything is available to you. Everything is to love. You are free. You are free to solely extend Love.

God is the pure Spirit that is Love. That that is unlike Love is fear. The part of your mind which you identify with in this world and have allowed to rule is the ego. The ego naïvely thinks it is separate from God and must direct its own course. The ego is God Itself using Its Power to create the perception that God is separate from God.

You are God who has and is Power and the power is always with you. You are limitless and free to create anything you desire. If you wanted to think you are separate from God just for the fun of it but could not, then that would be a limitation. As it is, your ego thinks it is separate from God and seeks limits of what is unlimited. God loves you and so It allows you to do this if you so choose.

Only the ego "needs" and "seeks". The ego is governed by fear. When lost in fear, it becomes unaware of Itself. The deeper the fear, the deeper your separation from God Itself. Therein lies the tragedy and comedy of you —God— to become aware again of Itself; to awaken to your Self.

Fear is false perception, thus errant thinking. Fear is what creates and sustains the illusion of separation. The ego is the culprit to the troubles you witness and experience in this false world it helped create. The ego makes you think you need to figure things out and do everything on your own. The ego is like the thief who stole your identity and cunningly seized your house key to the kingdom but you did not know it. It is trespassing in your home while you live homeless outside. The ego is an impostor. The ego is the false self. That is, it is the false you that you think you are and it is misleading you in this world.

There is much fanfare about killing the ego. I view this as nonsensical as it is contrary to Love. This is akin to doctors telling you to cut out the appendix. Because they do not know what it is for and see any practical function, they want to get rid of it. The ego is a part of you just as your hand is to your arm and you would not amputate it just because you perceive it useless or damaging to you. It is not a right, wrong, good, or bad thing. It simply is. It exists for reasons only God comprehends. Simply know that it is the aspect of your consciousness that unfortunately makes you think you are separate from God. It is just the mistaken identity of yourself. It serves you in other ways. Simply forgive it, which is forgiving yourself, and get on with it.

At this present moment, you may not grasp the significance of the perceived separation from God. Everything that is going on is about this separation. Understand well that in this "life", you are either increasing separation or correcting separation; you are either inflicting suffering upon yourself by separating yourself from God or you are healing yourself by unifying yourself with God. Your sole task or role is to recognize this separation and to correct it. The atonement is the one purpose. You are part of the one purpose —the transfiguration of human consciousness—.

On this physical plane, infants that are separated from their parents, particularly their birth mother, are known to suffer trauma. The repercussions resulting from separation at birth are well documented.

Everyone is a child to a parent. You as a child may admit that if you do not have a close relationship with your parent, you feel disconnected or lost somehow. You know not why but you feel a lack of direction. If this is true from the time of birth, then the sense of disconnection into adulthood becomes greater. You will have a persistent nagging sense of something missing in your life, of being unfulfilled. As such, you subconsciously and persistently seek to fill this void.

When a parent and child are separated, who feels pain and suffering? Both the child and parent feel pain and suffering. Why? Because the two are eternally connected. The Love between them is apparently broken. With no knowledge of the Truth, the illusion of separation exists. When a child and parent reunite, embrace and hold each other, they both feel peace again. You know this. You witness it readily in physical form when you see a child held in the arms of its parent.

You are not the body-mind. Imagine having awareness as you do now but you are without a body. You do this while you daydream, while you dream when you sleep, or while you sit and meditate. You are pure unlimited spirit who happens to currently have an embodied experience. That is all. The illusion of separation leaves you an inexplicable sense of emptiness that lingers. You can only heal when you restore your perfect union with God. That is, when you allow yourself to receive perfect Love.

The ego causes you to think that the world you see and experience with your physical senses is the conduit or means through which you gain all things such as Love, peace, joy and happiness. You are caught up in the perception that what you experience is coming to you from the outside and that you must therefore seek to adapt yourself to it and get things from it. This is reversed. In reality, you are the conduit through which all such things demonstrate itself in the world. Heaven then is the resulting world because you are the conduit through which the Mind of God flows. This is where the catch and the irony is. You can decide whether to continue the path the ego leads you or to think, approach, and act differently as God created you to be.

Fear and all its masks (ie. helplessness, hopelessness, despair, anger, hatred, envy, greed, et cetera) are all symptoms of a delusion that has occurred in the depth of the mind. All negativity is an expression of fear. This has occurred because you have not cultivated the skill of listening to the right voice of God within. Instead, you have cultivated listening to the wrong voice of the ego. You have not cultivated Love which involves allowing, embracing, and trusting the comings and goings of your experiences. Instead, you have cultivated fear spurred on by the ego who teaches you to strive, to seek, to control, to judge, to compare, and to pick and choose what you will be responsible for.

At this point, we make a very important declaration that, like the other declarations, you must be cognizant of always.

— You are cause and the world of form is effect. —

From the time of physical birth, you are caught up in the perception that what you experience is coming to you from the outside and that you must therefore seek to adapt yourself to it and get things from it. You are naïve to the fact that the world comes from within you; that the world manifests from your consciousness. You are cause and the world of form is effect.

You think you are the product of the world you see around you, the product of your parents, or the product of forces beyond your control. All the while, you are the product of yourself —your thoughts, beliefs, and perceptions—.

You are not dependent upon the world to exist. You exist in spite of it. The world depends on you. You are the Power and the cause and the world of ever-changing form is the effect. You are the Power —the consciousness that creates the world—. Without you to witness, perceive, or experience the world, the world does not exist. As such, the world means nothing and has no real power over you.

Your consciousness is a feedback loop or mechanism that allows you to witness the effects of the choices you are making in the depth of your mind. You do not experience objects but rather the effect of a thought or belief in objects. You do not need a body-mind to extend Love. The world of form is only the medium or means for your unlimited spirit of consciousness to experience itself. Look at the outcome in order to discover the thought.

The world is consciousness objectified. The world is innocent because you are the one responsible for creating it. The world merely serves as a mirror to reveal the extent of your God consciousness. You give the

Daryl Chang

world power over you when you —the false you that you think you are— mistakenly judge or perceive it.

You are not the body-mind. You are pure unlimited spirit who is unbounded and undefiled but potentially debased by the limiting thoughts, beliefs, perceptions, or things of the world. The mind that identifies with the world of form suffers from the illusion of fear. The Mind of God looks beyond all form and identifies with content only or simply the reality of Love.

The voice of the ego has led you to believe that your creations determine your worthiness, that your creations have power over you, and that your creations are outside of you. The ego has moved you deep into that consciousness that separates you further from God and Love.

Through the ego, you have become identified with your perceptions and experiences such that you think that these things are you. You have not cultivated the awareness that they are simply reflections of your consciousness. You do not embrace whatever arises. You do not let them go, particularly when you view them as negative.

Any feeling of need is driven by the ego —the false self— because it thinks itself separate from God. The true Self knows that you and God are one; that God is all in all; that we are all one; that all are equal; that no one is lesser or greater than another. Though some seem ahead or behind, all are pure unlimited spirit and have the same equal power and freedom to create.

The ego not knowing of its union with God needs to think and feel itself special. As such, it persistently contrasts, compares, judges, strives, seeks, and competes. It creates veils of dualities. It needs the car, house, boy, girl, title, fame, money, attention, happiness, peace, love, et cetera and so it strives, seeks, and competes for them, constantly judging and comparing itself to another. The belief in separation has created a black hole of endless seeking outside of itself not knowing that what it seeks is already within. It fundamentally does this because of fear.

The need to control is an effect of fear not Love. When you know you are always safe to feel whatever comes into your consciousness, then there is nothing to fear thus you need nothing.

All your perceptions and judgment arise from your ego. Judgment always creates separation. The egoic mind judges so that the dream of separation can continue. It needs the dream to continue to survive. Without judgment, without the dream, the ego perishes.

Judgment is a toxic act. It results in pain, sorrow, anger, despair, fear, ugliness, hopelessness, and all sorts of negative feelings. Judgment always creates separation and guilt. When you judge someone, you evoke a sense of guilt in that someone, even if that someone is yourself. You will affirm that person's lack of self-worth they are already feeling inside. When you judge anything or anyone, you elicit guilt within yourself too. Somewhere within you knows intrinsically that there is purity in your brother or sister and that you are not extending Love as you want to or should.

Your perception is you placing a value on your judgment of a person, experience, or whatever. The accuracy of your perception is influenced by the limiting beliefs and knowledge you have. If you reflect and are honest with yourself, you will admit that your perception of anything is always questionable.

You are meeting a friend for lunch at 12:00pm. It is now 1:00pm and she still has not arrived. In fact, she never shows up. You become annoyed because you perceive her to be inconsiderate and disrespectful of your time. Later that day, you learn that she got into a car accident and was taken to the hospital.

You have worked hard for the realization of an opportunity you truly desire. Your desire is not fulfilled. You are extremely disappointed because you perceive that another such opportunity is not possible. One week later, you encounter an opportunity far better than the one you sought and had thought possible.

You identify yourself as an environmentalist while another works as a lumberjack. Your perception of a tree will be different than the lumberjack's. You perceive the forest of trees as a habitat for wildlife that should remain. The lumberjack perceives the forest of trees as a means to make paper.

What is right and what is wrong? You are unable to state what is true and what is false. All events are neutral until you place a value on your

30   *Daryl Chang*

judgment because of fear which in turn unremittingly breeds more fear and then more judgment.

God does not judge. If God was to judge and perceive the correctness of Itself, then the Life that God is would cease to exist in the next moment and it would never be again. God is all-knowing and knows Truth —Love— is the only reality. When you know, you never ponder if a thought is true or correct. All thoughts are true and correct. Judgment is neither necessary nor relevant.

Now, we delve into aspects that demand greater thought and value.

One aspect is projection. Projection is an act of trying to psychically throw off what you do not want to own within or do not believe is inside you, particularly everything that you judge as being despicable or unworthy of you. Remember, nothing you experience is caused by anything outside of you. Projection is the denial of this truth. You are a creator who is powerful but projection implies that you are not powerful and that you are a victim. Projection is self-denial. That is, projection is you not acknowledging yourself as self-creating what it is that you do not want.

For instance, you encounter someone who is very critical. What typically happens? You judge and despise it so you "project" it. That is, you throw it back out angrily to that someone or whomever happens to be nearby. You believe that your anger is justified. You are trying to convince yourself that that darkness of criticism is not in you, it is outside of you. But the fact that you are reciprocating shows it is in you as well. It is ironic because both persons are projecting themselves onto the other, each thinking they are justified in their action.

Here is another example to solidify the understanding of projection. Think of a person, past or present, who you consider as being the greatest. Ask yourself, "How do I know that this person is the greatest?" You recognize and know it because that greatness is in you. How else would you know? Do the same now for someone you regard as the most evil. Ask yourself, "How do I know that this person is the most evil?" If you are honest with yourself, the very fact that you can react with knowledge that that is evil is because you have likewise been there in your mind. You may not act on the evil but the energy has come into your field of awareness, and you recognize and know it. How else would you know? You are trying to convince yourself that the evil is out there. It takes one to know one. You will concede then that you are a liar and a hypocrite. And so you learn to embrace every dark shadow within and without yourself. For Love allows all things, embraces all things, trusts all things, and thereby transcends all things.

Judgment and projection arise because of apparent fear. How so? You judge because you remember how hurtful you have been when you have acted from that energy. You judge harshly because you fear that energy in yourself. If you did not fear it, you would just let it be.

Who then is worthy of your judgment? No one. Who then is equal to you? Everyone. And who then is worthy of your Love? Everyone.

Now that we understand projection, we can better appreciate the aspect of forgiveness and the power it holds. We now make a declaration.

— Forgiveness is the key to self-Love and healing. —

Forgiveness is the riddance of perceptions, hence judgment. That is, to forgive means to release another from the perceptions you are projecting onto them. This includes perceptions you have of yourself. Forgiveness is the act of relinquishing what you decided is true about the person or the world. Forgiveness is the act of you not insisting on replacing Truth with your own version of it. Forgiveness therefore is an act of forgiving yourself of your projections.

When you have forgiven yourself, you will not react to another. You will feel the energy of the other, discern that energy, understand that energy, and you will see through it. You will think rightly with the Mind of God and see the face of God before you. You will have cultivated the ability to Love and naturally extend the Love.

Let us take a moment to get some additional perspective on forgiveness and to grasp further understanding of what it truly is rather than what you perceive it is. For it is the key to Love.

You typically associate forgiveness with wrongdoings only. You think forgiveness is required only when you perceive a wrongdoing is committed. This is a misunderstanding or misinterpretation. Everyone and everything requires your forgiveness, the release of your judgment and perception so that they remain pure and innocent as they are. It is your judgment and perception that colours the purity and innocence.

Forgiveness is often thought of as a release or relieving of guilt granted for a perceived sin committed; as a precious gift that you withhold from another who has wronged you and who you believe does not deserve it. If you believe someone has wronged you, even if that someone is yourself, then you have made a judgment. Judgment is the opposite of forgiveness. If you have not grasped judgment in the wholeness of your being, go back and read about it again.

If forgiveness is a precious gift that you hold, then why do you feel inner conflict, pain, and suffering? Is it fair that you should feel such if the sin is not yours? You think he is separate from you and has no influence on your thoughts, nor yours on his. Yet, he holds power over you, your thoughts, and your feelings.

Forgiveness, it seems, is regarded as an act that displays the specialness of the person who gives it in contrast to the one of wrongdoing and who receives it. That is, if you forgive another, even if begrudgingly, then there is an air that you are a better person to someone lower than you.

Everything is pure and innocent because you are the one who creates it all. All events are neutral until you make the decision what it will be for you. Forgiveness is the recognition that nothing has been done to you. In truth, you have done it all to yourself.

Thoughts of separation, judgment, and specialness are of egoic consciousness. You and God are one and you know that all are equal; that no one is lesser or greater than another. When you accept complete responsibility that you create everything, you see that the world is innocent and that all events are neutral. When you judge, you decree that the innocent are not innocent which in turn means that you yourself are not innocent. So forgiveness is you no longer substituting Truth with your version of truth which is founded in fear. When you judge, speak, or act other than from Love, you are the one that suffers for it. So recognize that forgiveness is a gift to yourself to feel Love and peace rather than self-inflicted pain and suffering.

When you forgive another or the world, you are reclaiming your power and realigning yourself with God. Another or the world can no longer hold power over you. You are saying, "I am using the power of Love to heal myself and the world. I am allowing, embracing, and trusting all things. I am bringing peace to this world and I am offering it to everyone." Forgiving another is not only an act of extending Love to another, it is an act of self-Love.

To forgive means to give it all up, to let it all go —the need to be right, the need to judge, the need to perceive, the need to rationalize, the need to refute, the need to be approved, and so on—. To forgive means to let go the thoughts of the person, the event, the world, whatever it is you think it is, whatever you think it is for, and whatever you think it has done to you. For in truth, you do not know what it is and what it is for, and nothing has been done to you. You have done it all to yourself. It is all of your making. You have created everything —the good, the evil, the anger, the sadness, the war, the peace, et cetera—. It is all you.

Practicing genuine forgiveness is essential. Forgiveness cultivates the quality of consciousness in which you finally come to forgive yourself and subsequently enhance your ability to Love. When you release all perceptions of yourself, you return from a limited self to the pure unlimited undefiled unbounded spirit that is Love, that you are.

God, Love, and forgiveness are synonymous. How so? Because there is no judgment, no perceptions, no projections; because each allows all things, embraces all things, trusts all things, and thereby transcends all things. Each sets all things free. Thus, when you are as God created you to be, you accept that you exist only to extend Love without attachment for Love is unconditional. You understand that if you are to create peace in the world, you must be at peace within yourself.

Now, we move on to the aspect of allowance.

Allowance is contrary to the actions of the ego. The ego that thinks itself separate from God is continuously striving. That is, striving for God, striving for perfection, striving for control, striving for things. Allowance is essentially the recognition that your life is no longer yours to dictate and control, hence there is no more striving. Rather, you have given it to the higher intelligence and wisdom —God— that knows best how to extend the Love that you are. Instead of judging, perceiving, projecting, and trying to control things, you cultivate the process of allowing.

Allowance is you leaving the things you see and experience to be and not react to them because you know that they are merely the effect caused by your mind and consciousness. It is you recognizing that the forms you see will arise and pass away as your thoughts change; that the forms are giving you feedback on what your predominant thoughts are; that the worldly forms have no power over you because it is you who has the power and brought them into existence of your awareness not the other way around; that the forms incorrectly gain power over you if you judge and perceive them thereby making them the cause and you the effect. Allowance is you maturing into the Truth of who you are and the power you are exercising to bring the world into form for your own experience. Allowance is you simply watching the movie you create play out in front of you, and simultaneously writing the script by changing the thoughts according to what you like or dislike. Allowance is the process of training your mind to be the Mind of God.

The ego will certainly resist because it is losing control. You, the false self that is you, is striving to get something that it perceives is lacking in yourself, whether it be a physical object or something like peace or happiness. The ego teaches you what to accept and what not to accept; what to take responsibility for and what to deny responsibility for. You will be disturbed by the tyrants who create wars and genocide. For what you cannot accept, you will judge. Then what you judge, you will not allow, embrace, or trust. Judgment and perception are actions from fear.

In allowance, you begin to cultivate an acceptance of all things in your experience. You see that the universe is conspiring to bring the people and events into your life that can best provide you exactly what you most need to learn or become aware of.

When you fully accept you and God are one, that you are wholly Love as you are created to be, that you create everything and that nothing experienced is outside of you, you will accept everything and forgive everything. Nothing is unacceptable. You will allow everything to be as they are.

For all the senseless situations, like war, poverty, and dis-ease, you need to first accept what already is. Acceptance does not mean you condone it. It means you rise above and understand it for why it is occurring. You are cognizant that the world is merely effect. You see that somewhere deep in your consciousness, you are not radiating Love but rather fear. You move beyond a negative reaction to a state of mind that begins to change it.

When you accept full responsibility that you are the one creating all your experiences, you will look with innocence, wonder, and disinterest upon all things. You will realize that when you look at another, you are seeing only yourself. When something in this world triggers you to be angry, stop right where you are and recognize that it is your egoic mind judging. Pause judgment and look upon it with innocence and honesty. Recognize that whatever triggers you with the greatest reactivity is the greatest seed potential of a learning opportunity for you; to learn about your greatest fear. Whoever triggers you with the greatest reactivity is likely to be the greatest teacher about yourself. Recognize that there is something you carry within you as a burden that you cannot forgive yourself. Recognize that each moment is to teach you Love, self-Love.

Now, we touch upon another aspect, that of surrender. Of surrender, we make a declaration.

— *Of yourself, you do nothing. God, through you, does all things.* —

Surrender is also contrary to the ego. The ego thinks it must control things; that it is making, doing, and living a life of its own on its own. Again, this is based on the perception of separation. That Life is separate from you. When you accept you and God are one, you will come to know that you are not living a life but rather Life is living through you. You will discover that God wants to direct and make Life through you. You will see and understand that of yourself, you do nothing. But God, through you, does all things. As such, you surrender. Surrender means you assume the role of a conduit through which the Mind of God, the Love of God, can flow and be expressed.

Surrender is essentially the fruit borne from you mastering allowance. Surrender is you wholly accepting that you and God are one; that you do nothing but God through you does all things; that you allow Love to flow through you by letting the Mind of God that has loving thoughts only direct you. Through your decision to remember only loving thoughts and to extend only loving thoughts, you allow God, the doer and maker, to manifest in the field of time, the expression of good and beautiful for your experience. Surrender is you becoming as the flower that allows God to do the work unimpeded thereby blossoming the unique expression you are and extending the Love.

The aforesaid statement may not make sense or be easy to accept as true presently. But this is just a habit from your egoic mind. You do not surrender by means of blind faith but through humility especially when your life is not to your liking or is a complete mess. Remember, you are completely responsible for all your experiences because nothing is caused by anything outside of you. If you are lost, sick, poor, and not at peace, why would you think or decide that you know how to create health, wealth, and peace? If you did, you would have accomplished it. If you are to find your way back, you must with humility accept that you can do nothing; that someone or something knows better and all. That said, you will admit, "I have done all this. No one is to blame. I must undo it. I must correct it. But I have no idea how I did this or how to undo it. Therefore, I must surrender to something else." That something else is the higher power, higher intelligence —*God*—.

Surrender is most challenging to the egoic mind that has tried to control everything forevermore. To take an initial leap of faith in it, you will need to make time to contemplate.

When a thought comes to you, you have rarely paused to ponder, "Where did that thought come from?" Many times a sudden random but inspiring thought comes to you but you dismiss it as imagination. A thought does not happen by accident. A thought is penetrating the conscious awareness from the depth of your mind that is linked to the Mind of God. The thought is the effect of God's will of Love entering your consciousness.

Though you are the literal creator, you are not the practical creator. You are a creator means that you create by being a conduit for Love, by allowing the Life of Love flow uninhibited through you, by allowing the thoughts you choose to flow through the mind and inside the depth of your consciousness, by witnessing the experiences that take form, and by extending Love. The thinking, doing, and making are the actions of God, the Supreme Intelligence that knows best how to bring the creations to form.

Surrender is you being willing to return to the state of emptiness where you are pure and innocent. You are empty of self, empty of striving, empty of the need to be right, empty of the need to judge, empty of the need to perceive anything in any certain way at all, and empty of attachment to the fruit of your actions. You recognize the voice of God guiding your personality, your emotions, and your actions. You discover that of yourself, you do nothing but through you, God does all things.

Learn to cultivate a childlike innocence and attitude toward all of your experience. Learn to ponder it, wonder about it, and not react to how it is getting you what you want or do not want. Embrace it and see what it is trying to teach you about your beliefs, your thoughts, your Self. Let it reveal to you how you are not seeing Truth and not being the Love you are so that you do see the Truth and be the Love you are. In allowance and surrender, you accept that God wants you to be happy and is always serving you what is best for you toward healing and the presence of Love. You cannot keep one foot in God's kingdom and leave the other outside and get to Heaven. All of your mind and energy must be committed to the presence of Love.

The seed that is put into the soil simply surrenders and allows God to work through it unimpeded. It needs do nothing. In time, it sprouts, breaks the surface, grows, and blossoms into the flower that it is. The flower does not busy itself with doing something in order to become something. It does not see itself separate from Life and so wants nothing of itself. It is one with what Life wants, which is nothing but to be. It does not judge itself whether it is beautiful or not. It does not ask or demand of another to tell it that it is beautiful. It senses, no matter how obscurely, its rootedness is in Being, the formless and eternal oneness of Life —*God*—.

If you pause to observe, you will notice a certain joy a flower somehow exudes just standing in the soil, doing nothing but simply being. At the same time, if you pause to observe yourself, you will notice you radiate a similar joy from doing nothing either but from merely observing it. Its essence —Love— is unchangeable and intangible and its existence is the extension of it for mere appreciation. At no time does it constrict the Love that is flowing through it. It does not judge the bee that hovers over it or the rabbit that chews on its petals. It allows and surrenders. You in turn reciprocate Love; you allow and surrender.

The flower radiates the natural harmony of the universe. Your inner spirit is filled with joy from the purity of this other creation you observe. The flower has not given you money to profit from; it has not baked you a cake to enjoy; it has not given you time to help you accomplish something; it has done nothing for you and asked nothing from you. Yet you are in joy. This is because it unconsciously reminds you of who you are and what you are ironically searching to achieve or restore —*Love*—.

      Daryl Chang

What would be the reason for the life and the beauty of a flower if there were no one to appreciate its loveliness? It would have no meaning here without you. Everything and everyone is a form for appreciation.

You see this flower you planted in your garden and recognize it as a rose, a name that was conveniently given by someone you know not. The ego smugly believes that because it can name what it is that it knows what it is and what it is for. You never really contemplate further. Do you recognize what was involved to bring it forth into creation and into your existence? How did it happen?

You may say, "I do know. I got in my car, drove down to the garden centre, paid cash for it, brought it back to my backyard, got a shovel out, and planted it." That is a superficial account of the rose which scratches but a tiny surface of its existence. You cannot find the moment in which that rose began to arise as a thought in someone's mind or that of God. You are completely unaware of the moment of the original birthing of the substance from which that rose has been created.

You must look at it with awe and recognize that it has come forth from the same mystery place as you, one that only God comprehends. You are in a sacred relationship with it for every relationship is a holy relationship. Every thing is a web of relationships. You are one with God and all. Ask yourself, "How and why did I call this object into my existence?" You can ask the same question of the car, the garden centre, the shovel, and so on. As you surrender to the awe of mystery, you will see that it was an allowance of God's Love to flow through all.

If you are still confused, resistant, or doubtful of surrendering to God —Love—, ponder these things that will bring you to humility. Do you know how to give birth to a solar system? Do you know how to give birth to the air you breathe? Do you know how you digest the food you eat? I can hear you say, "No!" Humble yourself to appreciate that you do not know anything. When you are in the state of divine ignorance, you will finally surrender and allow the higher power and higher intelligence God is to move through you and reveal to you all things.

Love pervades you. When you are not of egoic consciousness, you recognize that there is nothing you need and hence nothing to strive for. You need not do anything. What remains is simply being the Love that you already are. If you are like the seed and simply allow the Mind of God to work through you unimpeded and do what It does, then you would purposely blossom into the ultimate unique expression you are as does the flower from the seed. From the Mind of God flow thoughts of joy, peace, happiness, compassion, eternity, life, forgiveness, and all things good. Learn to cultivate and nurture within that Self only that which speaks of such things. If however, you stray and have unloving thoughts thereby restricting its flow, you compromise its beauty.

At this moment, you may have a sense of relief and lightness as if a burden has been lifted off you. That is because it has. You are like the homeowner who hired a contractor for free to renovate your home. You need not know how to use a hammer and a drill. You need not know how to install flooring, drywall, or the kitchen sink. You need not worry about the details on how you want your home to be. You need do nothing. You simply trust the contractor who knows how to do it, embrace him, allow and surrender to him to do the necessary work.

You are a conduit for Love. Of yourself, you do nothing. God, through you, does all things. You are the garden hose attached to the infinite water supply that God is and exist simply to allow Love to flow through you and express itself. When you water your garden with Love, your garden thrives. If instead you restrict your Love through contractions of fear, your garden withers.

As you learn to place less value in the things of this world, simplify the nature of your own consciousness, and surrender to that invisible spirit God is, you will notice a feeling of lightness or purity. It will be like you had a garage sale and got rid of stuff you finally realized you never needed in your home. When you learn to silence all your judgments, perceptions, and reactions that arise in your mind, you will become more of what God created you to be —the thought of perfect Love in form—. You will notice an inner peace and you will smile.

Here now, we introduce a very important notion that requires humility. It requires your astute attention and observation of its repercussions. Understand it well. The notion is this.

— You do not actually know what anything is for. —

All forms in your experience may appear different but they are all one; may appear to have a different purpose but there is but one. They are all attempts to awaken you to the presence of Love. You have only placed

Daryl Chang

value upon certain ideas and perceptions of what you think something is for.

Every time you judge someone or something, the judgment is always a present thing. So even if you make a judgment ten minutes ago or ten years ago, it will still remain with you. Once you bring awareness to it, it becomes a present thing. You are continually embracing and bringing your past to the present moment.

Say you are a scholarly squirrel who comes across a spoon in the garden. You look at it. You touch it. You smell it. You listen to it. You should admit that you do not know what it is for. You do not interpret, analyze, or judge the spoon. It is not necessary to know. You release it of your perception. You forgive it because you do not know.

So it is with all things that come into your awareness, including your brothers and sisters. Look upon anything with perfect innocence and naïvety as a child. You know nothing. You forgive it. God does not store perceptions and knowledge. Love keeps no records of wrongs for it judges nothing and does not bring its past with it to any moment.

Imagine coming across something completely unfamiliar to you. Be still in the stillness and noise of all that is around you. Be not influenced by surroundings, people, beliefs, perceptions, and past experiences. Do not let your mind stray or waver. Do not analyze, interpret, or judge it whether it be someone or something. Do not resist it. Admit your ignorance. You do not know what it is for. In that space, simply and deliberately forgive the creation. Bless it. Embrace it. Let Love flow through you unconditionally and thereby heal it. Let it go. Let it all go. Be this way with all encounters.

If you remain in the egoic illusion and see your brother or sister as separate from yourself, as someone to get something from, then you will not truly know what your brother or sister is for. In Truth, a brother or sister comes into your awareness to teach you one lesson —Love—. Their presence is to be loved, to be celebrated, to extend the good, the presence of you, God —*Love*—.

Now, let us explore creation a bit further.

Let us get additional perspective on what an extraordinary experience creating anything is. Baking a cake provides a perfect example. There are a lot of things happening you are not truly conscious of and take for granted. Though you are the apparent personal creator of said cake, there is truthfully just one Creator involved in the process of making the cake you desire.

A cake starts off as a bunch of individual ingredients which on their own are generally simple, common, and ordinary. Individually, you regard them as nothing special. You mix the ingredients together, process them in a certain way, and somehow it transforms into a perfect whole form completely unrecognizable from its originating elements — an uplifting experience—. However, use improper ingredients, incorrect quantities, combine them in the wrong way, process them in a haphazard way, and you produce a totally undesirable cake —a letdown experience—.

The ingredients, the measuring tools, the utensils, the pan, the oven, the recipe, and the electricity are all creations of other creators you have never met and know not the origin. You would not be able to bake the cake without them. When you place the cake batter into the oven at a set time and temperature, you hand over the remainder of the creation process to a Supreme Intelligence, the ultimate creator. You display a sense of belief and faith that the desired cake will result because you have diligently followed the recipe instructions. You set it and forget it. You surrender and simply observe the cake as it bakes. To continually open the oven door and check on the cake would affect the resulting cake negatively. Your cake indisputably would not come into fruition without the cooperation of ineffable others, particularly the Supreme Intelligence.

The creation process applies with anything you believe you personally create. Reflect on creations such as a garden, a baby, a beautiful and healthy physical body, a book or work of art, and you will concede the truth in this. Even when you create an inanimate object such as a coffee table, a cell phone, or a car, the Supreme Intelligence plays a part in the resulting practical function of it.

Everything you create in your life follows the same principle. The object of your desire, whether it is something you wish to be or have, is the cake. The ingredients, recipe, and process are metaphorically the same otherwise.

There is a point where once you combine all these dynamic ingredients, you must surrender the rest of the creation process to the Supreme Intelligence. In effect, you do nothing.

Let us look at four ingredients that are keys to the creation process and its relation to what we aspire —Love—.

The first key is desire. You are empty without desire. Desire initiates creative flow. Desire is the match that lights a fire in you to create. Desire is possibility seeking expression. All that there is of your desire is seeking expression through you. Desire is the urging of God. You allow desire to move through you and recognize that it is the voice of God guiding you to your atonement, your oneness with God.

With Love as the goal, desire then perfect union with God, to be all as God created you to be, even if you have no idea what that might be.

The second key is intention. Intention means to use your time wisely and persistently to focus your attention on the desire for Love. It means to not be distracted by things that take your focus away from what you desire. It means not being seduced by every distraction this world has produced that keeps you where you are and from advancing to where you want to be. Distractions can include things that may have become customary such as watching television passively, hanging out with friends to fill some time, or drinking at a bar to escape the weariness of the world. Intend then to practice newer habits that move you in the direction of that desire.

The third key is allowance. You recognize now that your experiences have been but reflections of your consciousness when you were unaware of your oneness with God. The world is the effect not the cause of your thoughts. Allowance is where you begin to cultivate an acceptance of all the things in your experience. You begin to view the events in your life now not as obstacles to getting what you want but as lessons to knowing the presence of Love. You begin to gain a greater awareness that you are not to control your life. You begin to trust more that higher intelligence that knows better than you.

The fourth key is surrender. Surrender means you begin to act only as a conduit for Love. You begin to choose only thoughts from the Mind of God to flow through you. You begin to accept the presence of Love that is. You begin to turn everything over to God. You begin to let

Love live and flow through you. You begin to notice you are witnessing the Life that consequently moves around rather than you busily doing things to make life happen as you think it should.

Here is an example or analogy that may help solidify for you the four keys aforementioned to the path of Love.

You are the gardener who desires to create a beautiful garden. From this desire comes the intent to use your time wisely to bring forth your desire. That is, you soften, sift, and till the soil; you pull up the roots of all weeds for you know that the effects of the weeds are no more thereafter; and you plant the seeds. You make sure that the weather conditions, the watering conditions, and everything is just right so that the seeds are well nurtured. You are simply preparing the place to receive the sun and rain of grace from God. You are cultivating the grace of allowing. Thereupon, you can do nothing but wait for grace to descend and so you surrender. The result of surrender: the petals emerge in their own time.

You may not see that the petals emerge because of all the things that have gone forth before: in the selection of the seeds, in the waiting for the perfect time to plant, in the daily cultivation and weeding of the garden. You may not see the causal connection. You will only see and witness the emerging of the petals. You, the wise awakened gardener, who is no longer fearful, have acted as a conduit through which there are no longer any obstructions to the offering of God's grace. You have opened and received the reality of Love for yourself.

You the gardener know you are only the keeper of the garden. Your ego does not swell. You bring forth the fruit which extends the beauty and scent of joy for all to see, receive, and marvel. The flowers, plants, vegetables, and fruits of the flourishing garden are not your possession but that which you have been given stewardship over.

Be therefore a wise gardener. Cultivate a deep Love and respect for yourself. Cultivate a state of consciousness in which the Love of God is unimpeded. All desires within you are gardens in which you prepare the heart and mind to receive the energy or power of Love that is freely given for the flowering of the soul.

In short then, your mission should you choose to accept it, is to desire the atonement, intend the atonement, allow transfiguration to occur, and surrender into the Truth. The mission is possible with willingness.

As we near the close of this section on awakening, we elaborate upon a few more vital attributes of God.

God is omnipotent, omnipresent, and omniscient. That is, God is all-powerful, all-around, and all-knowing. At this stage, one question may remain. That is, you may now be more accepting that you too are all-powerful and all-around. But how are you all-knowing?

True knowledge is that which does not change and is unchangeable: Truth, reality. Reality is Love for Love is reality. Anything and everything else is unreal or illusion, not true knowledge. Love is the essence of your being thus knowledge is the essence of your being. You are reality —Love, Knowledge—.

Know that when you say, "I do not know," your mind is not choosing reality. You are entrapped in egoic consciousness that is still seeking answers or knowledge. You are choosing to not be who you are and looking elsewhere other than within.

Knowledge is certainty. Knowing is a powerful state of consciousness. Know you and God are one. Know only Love is real. Know you are not alone. Know you cannot fail. Know you are safe. Know you are worthy. Know you matter. Know God loves you unconditionally. Know God supports you at all times. Know God provides you everything always. Know your happiness is God's will. Know you have the power to create whatever it is you desire. Know you are free. Know you have no need to survive and that you are free to extend Love. This knowing is true freedom to simply be as you are, to abide in your own nature, and to do what your heart desires.

You are one with God, the Source of creation. This means that anytime you have a situation where you need an answer or you need to make a decision, you have within yourself access to perfect knowledge. Perfect knowledge, perfect Love seeks to extend itself for that it is in its nature. You have already within the consciousness that is you, the answer for each question, problem, or decision you seek. The answer is one that helps to extend Love without condition or attachment, first into your own beingness and then through you to all.

Knowing is a great feeling. Knowing is so much better than not knowing, assuming, believing, and guessing. When you know, you feel and experience it throughout your body. You will be filled with joy.

Have no fear because God is always with you. God's will is for you to be happy and safe. You are always safe to do as you desire because God has and is the Power that makes it so. For this to be true always, you must simply know this. Not believe, hope, or have faith it is so but to know in your heart it is so. For it is Truth.

This may not be as difficult as you may make it out to be. In initial stages, you may have to have belief and faith in the truth of it but eventually, when you experience the results from knowing, you readily accept it as fact, a Truth. You accept it with the same knowing as when you were a pure and innocent child.

When you are a child, you inherently believe whatever your parents teach, tell, or say to you. When they tell you something —"you are beautiful," "do whatever you wish to do that makes you happy," "dinner is ready"— you accept their word. At no time do you doubt or question them. As a child, you did not necessarily have any belief and faith in them per se. You simply knew that what you were told was true.

You exhibit the same unwavering knowing when you visit a restaurant. After deciding what you want, you state your order to the waiter who tells you he will bring you your order. You never question thereafter whether your order will arrive. You have this innate knowing, possibly accompanied by belief and faith in him, that the statement is true. Everything is yours for the asking.

So it is with God. God provides you with everything with or without your need to ask. He unconditionally loves you and wants to give you everything and in fact, He has and He does. And just like your waiter, He is always there and ready to give you anything you ask. Everything is your inheritance. You are to simply know this.

God is pure, unlimited, eternal, and infinite Spirit so time does not exist. God knows neither beginning nor end. Time is linked only to form. The things of time are not eternal. All forms are birthed in time. What is birthed in time, in time, will end in time. You are not the body. The body serves as a temporary communication device in the world of form for the pure unlimited eternal infinite spirit that you are. The body is born in time and will end in time, the perceived death, but the essence of you —Love— remains.

The unawakened one who lives by illusion and all its forms will falsely suffer and experience death believing it is real. The forms of the world are a smokescreen. They are the colour, texture, and things you as an artist paint on the blank canvas that is Love. They are the musical chords and notes you string together and play amidst the silence that is Love. They are the actors and props you hire to act out the movie plot on the production set that is Love. No matter the painting, the song, or the movie you create, you love the creation because it was borne from a place of omnipresent Love that is you.

Love, the essence of God, of yourself is the only thing that knows neither beginning nor end. It is eternal. With this understanding comes the realization to see only content —Love— in everything and everyone, and not the forms they appear in. Content is primary and what matters, the form is secondary. The awakened one is always conscious of the Love that pervades all forms and knows death is unreal thus is free to freely extend Love. The awakened one rests in the perfect certainty of Love so deeply that the thought of restricting another's freedom cannot and will not arise.

God is perfect. God is in and is a perfect good state always. You are one with God. You are perfect. God is all in all. Everyone is perfect. Everything is perfect. The world is perfect.

You may not see the perfection of yourself and the world around you because you do not fully know who you are as yet; because you misperceive perfection; because you misinterpret or misunderstand the meaning of the word perfection.

You perceive you are not perfect because you perceive you are not whole and complete as you perceive God is. You are not always kind, calm, and good; you are judgmental, attached, and resistant to things; you make "mistakes" (ie. miscalculated your shopping bill, painted the bedroom the wrong colour, scolded your child for something petty, et cetera). You degrade yourself to mean personal failure or unworthiness exemplifying to some degree your lack of self-Love. Hence, you think and say, "I'm only human. I'm not perfect." You are wrong on both counts.

Let us say you want to make something such as a cake, a coffee table, or a romantic dinner. If it comes out exactly as you want, intend, or expect, then you say it is "perfect". If it does not come out exactly as you want, intend, or expect, then you say it is "not perfect". This is your current perception or interpretation of it. Perfection has no relevance to your expectations. In truth, it is "perfect" because the result is *exactly* as *you* created it, though unintentional intellectually. The floppy cake, the crooked table, and the disastrous dinner are also "perfect" because of what you did do based on your present mastery of its creation. The universe is a perfect mirror of you. So you see, you are "perfect".

As you progress to the Truth —of who you are, *God*; of being the actual sole creator of your world, your life; of the intent of all things in your existence and the purpose of all action— you will see and understand the perfection of everything in your world. Like the cake, coffee table, and romantic dinner, you create everything exactly in your world according to who you are and what you do, whether you are conscious or unconscious of it. The perfection of your creation corresponds to the mastery of your innate Power and Love. You create consciously or unconsciously non-stop and the result is the physical which timely reflects your God consciousness. It is your creativity in its current perfect form. You acknowledge and appreciate the moment-to-moment perfection.

Each circumstance, experience, and lesson is perfect for the growth, development, and evolution of yourself. Where you are in every moment is the perfect place for you to be. Every piece is a perfect fit to a perfect puzzle that is the unity of all life —*Oneness*. There is no-thing that is a personal "imperfection" or "failure". As you embrace more of this perfection, along with the awareness of connectedness, you will be less resistant to apparent adversities and integrate more effortlessly all of the life around you. You see that all is to teach you to fulfill the highest expression of the Divine presence within yourself. In so doing, you enhance the manifestation of good health, abundance, Love, peace, joy, et cetera for yourself and inherently mankind.

The ability to see perfection in all things may be instantaneous or it may be a gradual learning experience. If you fully grasp who you are – *God*–, you will have a true perception or perspective of perfection. If you do not, you will not. Conversely, if you have a true understanding of perfection, then it will help you to more firmly grasp who you are — *God* the creator—. Be flexible with the dynamic of the two.

If you say you know who you are —*God*— and you say, "I AM rich, healthy, and good," but then walk down the street and say, "I see a poor beggar, a sick man, and an evil person," you are still not who you intellectually think you are and are not seeing correctly. You are only as perfect as you perceive or know others to be.

If you see a sick person, pray and hope he gets better, you judge wrongly. If instead you see a perfectly healthy man (ie. you envision him as he ought to be —vital and strong— not as he misperceived himself to be), you discern correctly. This principle applies to any negative attribute (ie. poor, bad, evil, et cetera) you misperceive. You recognize the presence and perfection of God and do not dwell on that which is seemingly not whole or perfect.

Remember, you are cause and the world of form is effect. Change the conception of yourself and others and you will automatically change the world you live. When you appreciate the perfection of your circumstances, you then know to not try to change people. They are only messengers telling you who you are. Revalue yourself and they will confirm the change. By feeling the presence of God within you, you give glory of this indwelling presence to all. You reflect into the One Mind what you think and thus contribute to what others think.

God is all in all so It sees no evil or darkness anywhere for there is nothing but Itself. God is all-encompassing so It can have no opposite. You, when unawakened, deny yourself the Truth of who you are. God waits for you and your consciousness to recognize It as yourself and your all-in-all. God waits for you to love yourself and your world. God waits for you to see, believe, know, and accept your own perfection.

Life on Earth is full of paradoxes. When you are vulnerable and feel unsafe but allow and surrender, you become invulnerable and find safety. When you are meek but know Truth, you gain strength. When you give up control, you are guided. When you need do nothing, everything is done for you. When you let go the world, the kingdom opens up to you. When you detach from your desires, your desires come into fruition. What you resist persists; when you embrace fear, Love returns to you. When you stop trying to live a "life", the Life of Love will live through you. When you empty your Self, you become fulfilled. As you become less and less of what you thought you were, you become more and more of what God created you to be —the thought of perfect Love in form—.

When you awaken to the Truth and who you are, you know that self-Love is crucial to your healing. You no longer tolerate judgment in yourself —of anyone or anything— because you realize that you are self-inflicting pain and suffering from it. You decide to love yourself because you recognize that no one else will love you as much as yourself so you might as well. You see that Love is the only thing worth valuing, that Love is unconditional. You love so that you can simply abide in your own nature.

The Mind of God is aligned with all loving thoughts —thoughts of perfect Love, perfect fearlessness, eternal life, peace, joy, forgiveness, and all things good. It is empty of all thoughts and perceptions that are out of alignment —fear, death, anger, guilt, and all things not good.

The Truth is simple. Your awakening to the Truth will complete when you hold steadily within the mind: "Only Love is real. You are not the body but pure unlimited spirit. You and God are one. You are only Love. You are God in a unique form walking this Earth. You choose Love over fear under all circumstances, always. You are free as you are created to be."

Daryl Chang

Love makes you accomplish extraordinary things;
fear makes you do despicable things.

Love is the real power that unceasingly inspires;
fear is an illusion of power and can only rule through persistent force.

PART
TWO

The Dream

♦

As you progress further to know your divinity and assimilate the Truth into your Being, you will see that this world is one big lie. It is lies upon lies upon lies upon lies upon lies. You will see that this world is upside down, that it is reversed, that it is backwards, that it is insane, that it is the creation from fear, that it is diametrically opposed to God's Kingdom of Heaven —hell—. If the world was Pinocchio's nose, its nose would be far longer than the tallest sequoia tree.

You can readily observe many tactics that demonstrate that the world is constantly reversing in subtle ways if you pay close attention. Before, you were innocent till you were proven guilty. Now, you are guilty till you prove you are innocent. Before, you had to opt-in in order to explicitly give your consent to others. Now you have to opt-out to remove consent from others to whom you never really gave; they just conveniently gave themselves consent first to justify the opt-out action required. Before, you were healthy until nature proved that you were sick. Now, you are automatically considered sick unless you take fraudulent tests to inanely prove you are not. Before, you were sovereign with the birthright of freedom until you broke a man-made law. Now, you have increasingly restricted freedom until you unnecessarily protest for freedom to possibly be rewarded with some semblance of sovereignty that was originally yours. Whatever is not yet upside-down is being tactfully flipped so that it does not cause an immediate uproar from those unconscious. This way, there is minimal disruption to the process of sustaining this false world.

This world contains hatred, war and violence, people killing each other, intentional destruction of the planet, poverty, dis-ease, cruelty, anger, greed, envy, et cetera. You innately know and feel that all such things are not good and not right. You wish such things did not exist but they persist. You want better but you feel powerless to affect positive change on a global scale, yet alone your own individual circumstances. You think you are but just one person among billions and so you cannot affect the change you much desire. So you accept the societal norms of this world, follow them without question or dispute, and do what you do to get by.

You are mistaken. You have lost your way.

You are thinking and working in reverse. You are working from the bottom up rather than top down. You are driving in the wrong direction on the one-way road that leads to Heaven. You are looking down when you should be looking up. You are looking through the peephole of the door with a limited view rather than opening the door to see the vastness of what is out there. You are Love who has unwittingly chosen to dress up in a Halloween costume as fear on a daily basis. You are playing a game of 'hide-and-seek' with yourself. You are God pretend-playing to be other than God.

You have been misled, deceived, duped, manipulated, intimidated, bamboozled, hoodwinked, hypnotized, conditioned, and enslaved.

This insane world is built entirely on fear and has made life drudgery with meaningless purpose and about survival. It has kept you centred on the physical material world, separated you further from God, distracted you from looking inside and held you focused on the outside.

The world is insane because the unawakened one is insane. Love is not conditioned by the conditions of the world. Love conditions the world. You condition the world. Do not let this false world condition you to its insanity.

You heal yourself of the insanity of this world when you reverse the thought structure of the world within yourself.

Know that each of you who knows and lives Truth helps contribute to the collapse of this insane world. Envision a world with billions of awakened children of God who have mastered fear and Love, who truly relate to one another, who help heal illusion, and who extend the oneness of God's Kingdom. Imagine what it would be like to live in such a society where only Love, peace, joy, and true freedom abide. The very thought makes me smile.

Understand well all the things and workings of this current world. Everything is to eradicate God from you. Everything is to detach you from your spirituality and your consciousness. Everything is to make and keep you a slave to a false god. Everything is to separate you from every brother and sister, every creature, every thing of nature —the sun, the air, the water, the lands, et cetera—. Everything is to unceasingly separate you further from Truth and God. Everything is to keep you from remembrance of Truth, God, Love, and your Power.

Who is doing such "everything"? For the moment, let us not put a label on anyone in particular but instead refer to that "who" as "they".

They are quite clever.

They have created church and religion to successfully distort the image of God. Many know not that the true God is good; that God is within not without; and that the true God has been usurped by a false god. They have implemented endless propaganda to this date so that many no longer suspect their deception and elaborate schemes.

They have created numerous factions. They have fashioned atheists to not believe in God; agnostics to not know what to believe of God; and firm believers to believe in God outside of themselves and a God of their making. They have mixed lies with truths to create confusion and misunderstanding of God. They have shaped copious religions across the globe to compete and fight amongst themselves as to whose god is the true God. They have manipulated all to be pawns to unconsciously serve the false god in its fabricated and false kingdom.

As with religions, they have created numerous countries and developed allegiances to divide and conquer. They make you turn on yourselves. You participate in the conquering of yourself and others.

They have endlessly preyed upon your unconsciousness. They have deceived, misled, and trained you to look for God outside of yourself always and never to look inside of yourself; to look only at the physical realm and never at the spiritual realm; to customarily look at your neighbour with fear and hardly with Love; and to look to them for guidance and never to God or yourself.

They have created a system based on survival. They have created money for the workings of this system. You have never questioned the basis for it, the validity of it, or the false authority behind it. You have become an economic slave. Hence, you will never have true freedom. You are forever their slave.

Every creature on this Earth in its native state has economic freedom. Man is the only economic slave on Earth. They have deceived you to be such through unnatural wants and acquired desires. They perpetually seduce you with images of glamorous lifestyles of actors, celebrities, and athletes. You fantasize and strive for the same. When you are unable to, you judge them to have more skills, gifts, and talent than you and that you are incapable of greatness yourself. Your unconsciousness is the bonds and chains that bind you, who are the slaves of want and desire.

They have tricked you into their game of commerce through the use of fictional identities because you know not who you are. You have bought into this game of survival based on money, an idea of value deeply implanted into the unawakened mind as a life necessity. It has been perverted so much as to have unyielding power. You are enthralled by its power. You fight against another robustly so that you can have more than the other. You can never have enough of it. You beckon to its call automatically and yet you are not any happier for it. You have been told a lie that the world is running out of everything. They have distorted abundance into scarcity and you have unwittingly bought into it.

Money is quicksand. The more you get sucked into its vortex, the more anxious, the more hurried, the more stressed, and the more depressed you become. Their economic system has engendered you with selfishness and greed rather than generosity. You may be capable and competent to do anything but you excuse yourself from your capability and competency to do it because there is no money in it; because nobody will "pay" you for it. Many times you have the intention of creating something "good" but it never happens because you get stopped in your tracks by "Where am I going to get the money?"

Now that you have made money your master, they have conveniently created banks and financial institutions to control money. You have given them the key to your control as their eternal economic slave. They implement worthless programs with labels like RRSP, TFSA, and high-interest savings accounts under the sham of maximizing your money to keep you tied to their system. They have falsely self-proclaimed authority and capability to seize your money if you are a disobedient slave. They have created an unsuspecting army of soldiers under the guise of employee roles. Government administrators, police officers, financial advisors, tellers, and bank managers, are the gestapo who blindly obey orders to control their fellow brothers and sisters who play the customer roles.

They have created lotteries with the fantasy of acquiring lots of money if you are "lucky". They have made you believe that abundance is not your natural state and that you must gain it somehow from somewhere outside of you. They keep you in a mindset of scarcity.

There is no legitimate ownership of so many things on this Earth (ie. land, air, water, et cetera) because they do not exist through anyone's labour. They stole it and it happened by force and manipulation without any regard but for themselves. They made laws to legitimize their ill-gotten gains. They have twisted things to suit their perceptions, to transform a right into a benefit into outright ownership. They have fooled all of us into perpetuating the crime.

They have deviously made everything a commodity —water, air, animals, food, nature, et cetera—. Even your own person, your own body has been commoditized. Everything is monetized and has a price, otherwise it cannot be obtained. Life is a consumer item.

They have cunningly formed a clandestine alliance that self-acclaims itself as a legitimate authority over all. They have tactfully set up a worldwide survival system of countries, banks, money, corporations, governments, churches, organizations, institutions, libraries, medicine, entertainment, law, property, media, and schools in society. They have infiltrated and commandeered much of the entire system now in place, set themselves into positions of false authority, and direct the slaves of the system. The entire system is fraudulent and rigged for their benefit. This alliance is the epitome of the Mafia but conveniently legalized by the main system of their own making. You are extorted, abused, and harmed if you do not obey and comply with any of their rules and pay up with the money they invented as a means for survival.

They have invented science, much of which is based on false premises, to play God in pretence of discovering Truth for mankind. They have claimed whatever God is and has as theirs —the lands, air, water, people—. They have taken ownership of all that God generously gave you. They have removed your God-given freedom in subtle fashion and self-proclaimed themselves as your god. They have rewarded you morsels of freedom to give you the impression they are kind gods to do so and you have believed them.

Daryl Chang

They have made a science of everything and conditioned you to believe they know better than God, the Source of creation. They have conditioned you to want and need proof from their scientists to believe anything and to not believe anything of God.

They have created subjects or studies to weave the stories they wish for you to believe. They have invented economics, the science of poverty, which has filled the world with more wretchedness and want. They have invented medicine, the science of dis-ease, which has increased dis-ease. They have invented religion, the science of sin, which has promoted more sin.

They ensure that your physical and mental well-being is always compromised without your knowing. They wreak constant havoc on your entire body. When you are in pain, you cannot think properly. They make you dwell upon sickness and death under the pretence of caring for your health and life. They pollute the air in pretence of fumigating germs that they have made you believe make you sick. They contaminate the lands and water with chemicals, pesticides, and synthetic fertilizers in pretence of human safety. They poison the foods you eat with artificial colours and flavouring, and man-made chemicals under the guise of preservatives. They genetically modify foods under the guise of better or improved foods. They make you dwell on disaster and buy into the need for insurance.

They have created a pharmaceutical industry consisting of doctors and hospitals. The medical system is the epitome of the drug cartel that is conveniently legalized by their main system. If you have a medical designation, you are coerced to be a drug dealer and follow their instructions on how to serve customers regarding so-called health even if harmful. You are extorted if you do not obey and comply with any of their rules. If you are outside their medical realm, you too are extorted and abused for you are not a drug dealer of their choice.

When you are sick from their making, they secretly poison you more with their bogus science, unnatural medicine or concoctions, and hypothetical advanced treatments. There are boundless dis-eases that conveniently coincide with the birth of their pharmaceutical industry and never really existed prior. They tout their treatments as the best cures and means for a dis-ease they help caused. There are lots of alternatives existing out there to treat such ailments. Many who are afflicted with dis-eases are conditioned to not look elsewhere because of the propaganda on the mainstream media they are solely exposed to. Furthermore, they have made you believe that illness and dis-ease are normal aspects of aging and life. You have believed them to expect it especially in old age and so you fulfill the expectancy.

They have created fake charities, establishments, and causes to give the illusion they are fighting for cures for ailments they helped produce. They are interested only in the sustenance of dis-eases because it means more customers and more profits in their survival system. Those involved in these establishments including participants of events raising funds for cures are all unwittingly part of the charade.

They have created a legal system to fittingly play god in the charade of protecting mankind. They have created its own language so that it is complex, incomprehensible, and perplexing to navigate. They have created lawmakers and lawyers so that you are dependent on them to interpret laws of their own making to their own benefit and liking. They have craftily written laws to mainly protect themselves not you as you perceive; have conveniently changed them based upon their dogmatic beliefs and personal whims; have forced them upon you to comply through the fear of punishment. They have intermingled lies with true facts to create confusion and doubt so that the baby is thrown out with the bathwater.

The legal system takes the act of projection and the need to judge, to make it okay socially so that you need not be concerned with this other as your brother or as your sister who has been crying out for help. Rather, you become justified in punishment. Yet punishment is only the insane attempt to convince the punisher that the darkness, the evil — whatever you want to call it— is not in them but that it is out there.

They have created a media industry that allows them control of the news and information disseminated to the public mainstream. The news on radio, television, newspapers, and magazines are verbatim yet it hardly evokes suspicion. The unawakened absorb their propaganda, blindly accepting information given to them as true, never venturing elsewhere and rarely accepting any new knowledge that is contrary. It has proven to be a reliable means to continuously generate fear and direct society.

They have created an education system consisting of schools, colleges, and universities. They dress up their teachings as a necessity to do and

Daryl Chang

be what you want, to get a job to work at, to earn more money, to achieve success, to do something with the life you live. In truth, they are indoctrination camps to stifle your own independent creative thinking, to program you to think what they want you to think, to train you to be obedient, to follow instructions without question, to use your body and mind to develop ideas and things for their own use, benefit, and advantage, to enslave you and to train you to enslave your brothers and sisters. You are a dog in their obedience school learning to sit, roll over, and play dead when commanded.

They have developed and orchestrated all things for war under the charade of protecting and enforcing peace: weapons of all sorts —guns, bombs, bioweapons, et cetera—; roles of all sorts —police, soldiers, armies, et cetera—; reasons of all sorts —enemies, histories, evil, et cetera—. The blatant contradiction should make it very unmistakable that it is not for peace but strangely it does not invoke suspicion to present day. War is a very effective and efficient way to generate and sustain fear.

They have created circuses in sports and entertainment to keep you amused, appeased, and distracted. The sports and entertainment industry is the epitome of prostitution conveniently legitimized by their main system. Athletes and celebrities are highly paid prostitutes that are conveniently legalized by their main system. The league and team owners are their pimps. The pimps are using the bodies, skills, and talents of their prostitutes for their own selfish gain. The athletes and celebrities think they are handsomely paid but it is pittance to what the pimps get. As prostitutes, they have to obey and comply with the pimps' wishes and rules, otherwise they receive punishment, which ironically, they have agreed to; they are expected to perform any requested acts like monkeys without objection even if it against their will, desire, or values.

Many sports are mainly violence that are packaged as games so that it is socially okay. Hockey, boxing, and UFC are the obvious examples. If two individuals in public fight, it is indicative that they mutually agreed to do so. The act of projection has reached an ultimate level whereby violence erupts. Because it is in public rather than a sports arena, it is judged as unacceptable. Society has deemed the need to judge here and invoke punishment to those involved. Meanwhile, in a hockey context, boxing ring, or fighting cage, a fight is judged as okay and warranted. The participants engage for an agreed time and resume life once time expires. The players are used as commodities as cocks in a cockfight. The owners amuse themselves because they are unhurt. The prostitute players show no indignity themselves because they think they are paid handsomely.

Violence within sports is supported, condoned, encouraged, tolerated, and rewarded. The fighters are praised for their behaviour and actions. In fact, they are idolized. Even those with skill and talent have to contend with possible injury from violence that has nothing to do with the game itself. Violence has been wrongly equated with toughness. In truth, to restrain from violence is to demonstrate mental toughness.

Sports fans are equal to task in promoting violence. They have been seduced to love it. It is convenient to love it when you are a spectator and not a direct recipient of it. They are beneficiaries like the pimp owners who enjoy it from afar without risk of injury. Fans accept violence as part of the game, learn to enjoy it, and almost beg for it. The league owners dismiss player safety and happily oblige as it proves more profitable. Unawakened parents normalize their children to it.

Sports fans develop a fanaticism that deepens their egos, as well as the egos of athletes they idolize. The concentration and potency of invisible negative energy of fear from the violence on the playing field spreads into the audience. Spectators are drawn into that field energy of fear and exhibit the same violent behaviour though they are not actually playing the game. A full-blown war at a soccer game develops because it is a forum for violence posing as an innocent game.

They have seduced you to enjoy violence as a pleasurable pastime. You willingly seek it out in video games, movies, sports, entertainment, news, et cetera. You rationalize it. You revel in it. You have been conditioned to love a "good" fight, an oxymoron.

Movies and television shows are presented as entertainment so that they are socially okay but are programs to "program" you. They have used it to tactfully plant the seeds of their creative thoughts into your mind to evoke the desired emotions within you, to instill more fear and feelings that are unlike God into you, and to help fulfill their impure desires. Horror, violence, evil, and fear are prevalent elements and intensified for epic products. Art imitates life and life imitates art, both feeding each other to regenerate, recycle, and replenish fear energy.

The entertainment industry of actors, singers, and musicians follow the same footsteps as sports athletes, selling themselves. Celebrities like their sports colleagues must obey and comply with the wishes of the media moguls. Tantrums and bad behaviour are emphasized often and rewarded nonetheless. Entertainment fans exhibit the same fanaticism as sports fans and make idols of them. The fans think them special and celebrities in turn think themselves special. Their egoic arrogance has let it all go to their heads. They have claimed their success as their own forgetting that it is because of God not themselves; that of themselves they do nothing but God through them does all things.

They have created addictive substances such as alcohol and cigarettes, conveniently legalized by their main system, that impact your physical and mental well-being. They have crafted the impression that they are for your pleasure. When your health is compromised, you then believe you need their treatments disguised as health measures.

They have created systems to track and monitor you, their slaves, of your whereabouts and in everything that you do; for without knowledge of you, you cannot be a slave for them. They have created churches where you voluntarily register your marriages. They have created hospitals where you voluntarily register birth certificates for your children, giving them ownership of your children. Each unsuspecting parent perpetuates the system for their manipulation. They oblige you to acquire licenses of all sorts. They have created passports for traveling; even a squirrel has more freedom to go wherever it wants to. They have created tax and revenue offices to track and monitor the status of their slaves. They have enticed you with scraps of illusions under the facade of child and spousal benefits. When you register for anything or agree to their scare tactics in their fraudulent system in order to do anything, and you rationalize the actions through fear, you imprison yourself further. You have agreed to their jurisdiction thus given them power to punish you when you disobey their rules.

They have created and seduced you with convenient digital systems and technologies such as credit cards, debit cards, and loyalty cards that allow them to track your money behaviour. If you were to spend cash person-to-person, they cannot trace you and dictate your behaviour otherwise. Notwithstanding, this is still based on their survival system.

They have created DNA services as another means to track you under the sham of helping you determine your ancestry. You have been preyed upon and seduced by your curiosity. You have freely given them your DNA thereby reducing their time and effort to locate you should you ever be a disobedient slave; to eradicate your race should they deem you unneeded anymore; to harm you with target specificity.

They have created advancing technologies with invasive frequencies that negatively affect your well-being without your knowledge. You are seduced by radioactive devices such as cell phones, fitness wear, wireless headphones, and microwaves as conveniences.

They cage, abuse, and mass kill animals for pleasurable consumption beyond satiation. They exploit animals for testing in the name of human safety. They confine animals into unnatural environments in the likes of zoos, aquariums, and safaris in the charade of science and entertainment. No other creature does such things to other creatures.

They destroy forests and lands of nature's habitat to other creatures in the pretence of food systems and economic growth. They have claimed many lands and natural resources to control the food and water supply systems they have built. They have made people dependent on their systems enabling them to control the supposed needs of survival.

They have cunningly manipulated your mind to separate yourself from animals and all of nature. You were then susceptible to separate yourself from your fellow human being. They desensitized you. Just as they had done with the animals, they extended it to humans so you did not notice. They cage your brothers and sisters as inferior prisoners. There is prevalent human and sex trafficking, particularly of the most vulnerable, children. Furthermore, there is known organ harvesting. There is complete disregard for the sanctity of life.

They are constantly training you to be evermore lazy, self-irresponsible, and dependent on others. They are cleverly getting you to unwittingly relinquish more of your personal power. They seduce you with conveniences like driverless cars, touch-less payments, and delivery services of all kinds. They cunningly eliminate physical contact of any kind to train you to eliminate spiritual contact too.

They have created work and societal roles so that all work is executed for them. All are pawns, puppets, and slaves in their system. The art of projection and the need to judge so that it is socially accepted as normal is everywhere: at schools between teachers and students, at home between parents and children, at work between employers and employees, at stores between staff and customers, et cetera. All brothers and sisters judge, perceive, project, and act as gestapo toward their fellow brothers and sisters. This is all to their benefit.

At a hospital, doctor and nurse roles serve the patient roles. At a police station, officer roles serve citizen roles. At churches, pastor roles serve patron roles. At government offices, tax collector roles serve taxpayer roles. At the retail store, cashier and sales associate roles serve customer roles. At banks, teller and financial advisor roles serve money collector roles. At law offices, lawyer roles serve law abiding citizen roles. At courts, judge roles serve criminal roles. At schools, teacher roles serve student roles. There are endless societal master and servant roles. They have ingeniously built a monstrous well-oiled, self-propelling machine fueled by the energy of fear. All involved are pawns and puppets orchestrated to do their dirty work to keep the gears of fear moving and self-proliferating.

They have created and twisted holidays and occasions to separate you further from God. They have made you forget the celebration intent of Christmas and commercialized it. The significance of the birth of Jesus Christ is overshadowed and lost through materialism. Like Christmas, the significance of Easter and its teachings of Jesus Christ are lost through the commercialization and material fun of Easter egg hunts and cute bunnies; through their distorted religious interpretations. They have beguiled you into Halloween as a fun event to dress up in cute costumes thereby allowing them to introduce elements unlike God. They have seduced you to enjoy it as a pleasurable occasion where you willingly revel in the images of death, horror, and evil; you elicit and delight in fear; you groom children to those things unlike God thereby raising more soldiers for their use. Through it, they have also enticed you to consume more of their toxic substances as food. They have hypnotized you to these things unlike God as cool. You wear, collect, and emblazon them as symbols of your specialness. You even tattoo yourself with them.

They keep you overwhelmed, busy, stressed, confused, and engender fear and anxiety to keep you in survival mode, and make you feel exhausted and defeated. They ensure this by making society run 24/7. There is no day of rest. There is continuous television and media — hypnotic devices— to spread their propaganda. There are work shifts round the clock. There are systems within systems to work through.

There are piles and piles of paperwork and useless details with every task or service. Much of the activities you do nowadays (ie. movies, music, alcohol, drugs, et cetera) whether for social, entertainment, or amusement purposes as you perceive, is really a means to escape pain, thought, or the life you deem normal.

They have you thoroughly focused on death. Alongside churches and hospitals, they have built old age residences, long term care facilities, and funeral homes to hoodwink you into believing in aging, physical/mental/health problems and death. They have cunningly imprisoned and trapped you in the physical realm identifying with the body to distract you from the spiritual realm and knowing you are pure unlimited spirit.

They do not want you mentally and physically stimulating yourself from spiritually within. They seduce you with mental and physical stimulation outside of yourself. They do this with movies, sports, music, video games, social media antics, and reality shows. You are continuously looking outside yourself at others, comparing yourself, and thinking you are incapable of more.

They want to keep the unconscious soul focused on the outer physical realm never to ponder and seek the inner spiritual realm. They create physical disasters and atrocities. They seduce you with all things that can appeal to your physical desires and pleasures like smoking, drinking, and watching pornography. They bombard the entire landscape with images of bountiful hedonism.

All that they do is for the purpose of incessantly increasing separation – separation from God and your neighbours. They inundate you with ideas, images, and illusions of good versus evil such as portrayals of superheroes and villains, police and criminals, democracy and communism. They inundate you with steady propaganda of dualities or polarities by cunningly providing illusions of choice such as liberals or conservatives, medicine or sickness, education or manual labour. They flood you with the unvarying message that you must compete and fight and that one must win (at all costs) and another lose; that you must be better and more special than another through sports (individuals and teams), employee positions, and reality shows about survival of the fittest. They do all this to keep you in judgmental and critical mode, and to generate hatred for self and others.

They intentionally create a relentless noisy and distracting environment so that you cannot hear the still small voice of God. There is never-ending noise produced from television, music, traffic, sirens, horns, debates, disasters, war, and global conflicts. The noise and distractions keep your mind full, cluttered, and unthinking.

In present day, they enforce lockdowns and social distancing under the fabricated guise of health and safety to ceaselessly increase separation. They endeavour to retard any encounters between an unconscious soul and a conscious soul thereby reducing the possibility of any awakening. They enforce face masks so that persons are faceless to eradicate warmth, visual display of positive emotions, and general humanness.

They have trained you very well to keep your distance from your fellow human being even before this manoeuvre. They have trained you to ensure you keep yourself separate from another; to see your brothers and sisters as dreadful strangers to be feared; to lose your divinity and humanness. They have trained you to not openly and willingly give help to or receive help from a random soul.

They have made you learn to live from fear, to think negative thoughts, and to believe the opinions of the world mean something. In so doing, you have conveniently created a world in which people are negatively minded, do not want to support you, and do not think you are worth anything. But this has resulted because you are the one projecting that belief about yourself.

They do all these things so that you look to them as god your saviour and to never look within. The unconscious soul has been forever hypnotized. They ensure that you do not have time to contemplate God, Love, Life, and who you are. They have conditioned you well to distrust those who tell you that God is within.

They will not stop and never tire till you are wholly removed from God. Consequently and conveniently, they can intimidate, manipulate, and enslave you along with the unawakened masses for their selfish motives. They have power only because you and other unawakened souls who do not know who you are, give away your power. They do so with the illusion of power when really they have none. They have the illusion of power because of the illusion of fear. Fear is the illusion of power and can only rule through persistent force which you are constantly under.

You have falsely believed in the workings of this world as necessary because you are in fear —fear of your brothers and sisters, fear of harm, fear of punishment— so you blindly follow man-made rules and laws from false illegitimate authorities. They have convinced you that all their laws, policies, rules and regulations are for your security and protection and you have believed them. You have willingly allowed them to restrict your freedom and aided them in enforcing and persecuting your brothers and sisters who fight for the freedom you give away. You do not question the validity of these things that you mindlessly obey. You are born free but you give away your freedom because you have been instilled with fear. You do this because you do not know the Truth of who you are.

They generate and use fear as an energy tool to keep you deeply occupied in their world. You fear parking tickets, interest hikes, and stock crashes. You fear thieves, lawyers, policemen, and government. You fear fires, earthquakes, hurricanes, and tornadoes. You fear war, poverty, dis-ease, prison, and death. You fear people, animals, insects, and germs. You fear losing your job, your home, your spouse, and your child. You fear honesty, criticism, competition, and judgment. You fear not fitting in, not standing out, and standing out. You fear being alone, not being approved of, and not being special. You fear missing out on sales, events, and friend gatherings. You fear the sun, the water, and the air will harm you. You fear embarrassment, failure, and success. You fear the past, present, and future. You lay fear upon fear upon fear like toppings on a pizza. You have learnt to fear something, anything, and everything. On and on and on it goes.

You do no harm, do nothing wrong, and do nothing at all, and yet you are in fear. You inarguably have a nagging unsettling feeling always. You have a constant nagging feeling at the back of your mind. You are in fear of being punished for breaking some silly man-made rule or law made by a false illegitimate authority. You are in fear that something bad will happen to you and not be able to rectify it. You worry about everything because you are in fear —fear of death and survival, of not having enough money to pay for events, fines, punishments, or future needs—. You embrace fear, do not know why, and do not pause to question why. They engender, teach, and instill fear purposely to keep you in fear. They prey on your unconsciousness. There is no freedom where there is fear. All this because you identify with the body and this is because you know not the Truth, the reality, and of the power you have but give away. You forget you are pure unlimited spirit. If you know you are God or Superman, would you be in fear?

The things of this world come not because you have perceived them outside of you but because you have allowed them inside the depth of your consciousness. You have allowed fear and all its derivatives to defile all that is pure within you. The Truth is simple. You are wholly Love. There is nothing to do but be Love and to love. When Love is not present within you means that you are in fear. At the moment you have allowed fear in, you have fallen back into illusion, into insanity. You are God suddenly forgetting who you are and choosing to act contrary to your Self.

Whenever you feel fear, particularly when it reaches a peak of intensity, pause or stop. Tell the Truth about it. That is, you are the Power and the presence of God, of Love creating it; that it is not real; that you made it up; that you created it out of your own consciousness. For instance, if you erroneously think you are alone, unloved, or unworthy, stop and tell the Truth about it. That is, you have misused your power; you are not alone; you are loved; you are worthy. Reclaim your Power and feel Love coming back into your being. Let Love satiate your Being till it overflows.

They have successfully turned you into a human battery of fear energy. You have become a negative energy cell that provides power to this false world. You are the dirty energy that pollutes and darkens the environment in which you live. Imagine if you transformed yourself back to a human battery of Love energy that instead powers God's true kingdom. You are then clean energy that purifies the environment. You produce fresh air that you can once again breathe and live in. Imagine billions of awakened children of God who provide the sustainable and renewable free energy of Love. There would be a billion watts of Light shining the entire universe. No one ever need be lost again for the path home would always be clear to see then.

Those who exhibit and act in any negative manner such as great anger, envy, hatred, greed, impatience, despair, worry, anxiety, and depression, do so because of immense fear. The greater the fear, the greater the pain and suffering. They who are vigorously trying to control, possess, or limit everything are those who feel emptiness. They lack Love and require the most Love. How so? Because Love allows all things, embraces all things, trusts all things, and thereby transcends all things.

Love sets all things free. Love is satiated in its own being. Love overflows. The tyrants, dictators, and oppressors have a deep hole in their hearts void of Love and filled with intense fear. They are extremely lost souls incessantly seeking to control because they indeed know not that what they seek is within. Think tenderly about this statement.

But the world that has them is just a reflection of social consciousness as a whole so the fault is not theirs alone. Oppressors and slaves are co-operators in unconsciousness, and while they seem to afflict each other, are in reality afflicting themselves. Think well about that statement.

You have no need to fear however. The workings of this universe are choreographed with elegant precision, unfaltering intelligence, and deep wisdom. God loves you and Its will is for you to be happy. When you are in perfect alignment with God, then Love, peace, and joy will blossom because Love allows all things, embraces all things, trusts all things, and thereby transcends all things. The world is not your means to Love, joy, peace, and happiness. You are the means through the Love you extend to bring Love, joy, peace, and happiness to the world and yourself.

When you are struggling with any negative issue, big or small, do not busy yourself with trying to find causes and solutions of physical means for this is ineffective and inefficient. Never identify yourself with your doing but let your doing be infused by your being. First understand the Truth and reality of your divinity. Then let yourself be guided by Love to take the necessary actions for your healing.

Understand well that when you are unawakened to God, Love, Truth, and your Self, you are then in a dream or sleep state. You will be a pawn, puppet, and slave in this false insane world. You will be incessantly in fear more than your natural state of Love. You will imprison yourself to the whims of others. You will be easier to indoctrinate, manipulate, deceive, intimidate, and control. You will act as a slave in your defined role in this organized system we call society. You will unwittingly enslave your brothers and sisters to the delight and benefit of the masters and owners, who are slaves themselves answering to a false god. You will be an active participant and accomplice to the insanity of the world, partaking in the evil, and perpetuating the crimes. You will think and believe not but you are.

Daryl Chang

The only relationship that holds any value at all is your relationship with God, your creative Source, the breadth of the sun of which you are a sunbeam. It is foundational. When this is in alignment, all of your creations, relationships, and actions will flow effortlessly.

Remember "need" is an expression of the perception that there is something you lack. This world is governing your beliefs that you need to be a certain way, that you need to be acceptable to others, that you need to conform and fit in, that you need to dress the way others dress, that you need to make money, and that you need to survive.

You need to get out of bed because you need to go to the office because you need to work at a job you do not particularly like because you need to earn money because you need to buy food because you need to eat because you need to live because you need to survive.

You need to sing and make lots of money more than anyone else in the world because you need to be famous because you need to feel special because you need to show you are better than your brother or sister because you need to know that you matter because you need that feeling to survive.

You need to bomb and kill all your brothers and sisters of that country because they made you believe they are evil and because you need to kill them first before they kill you because they are the evil ones not you, even though you have never met any one of them personally, because you need to survive.

You need to inject an unknown substance into the body because they made you believe you need it to survive. You need to inject an unknown substance into your brothers and sisters which will harm them because you need to do and keep your job because you need the money to pay your rent because you need a place to live because you need to feel safe because you need to survive.

You need to honour your parents. You need to make everybody happy. You need to survive. Whoever told you that you need to do such things? You need do nothing. It is quite different to want or to choose to do something. When Love is operating, you naturally want to or choose to do something. The feeling of need is not necessary, relevant, or considered. The power of freedom to choose and to create what you desire exists when you are not governed by need, by the belief of the world that you must be a certain way and do certain things. There is no freedom where there is need.

You need to defend your point of view because you need to be right. "Need" becomes a black hole of insanity borne from an illusion of fear.

When you pause to reflect, the impact of neediness is self-evident. Ask yourself, "How do I feel when I am around or with someone who is "needy"? How do I feel when I am around or with someone who is "not-needy" but loving?" Then thoroughly think about how you are when you are the one who is needy or when you are the one who is not needy but simply loving. One way of being is exhausting and the other exhilarating, is it not?

All is God. God is all. When you look at your brother or sister, you are looking at yourself. When you judge your brother or sister, you are judging yourself because you are the one who is creating all of your experiences. No one is lesser than another or greater than another for all are equal.

When one is rich with one million dollars while another is in debt of one million dollars, it does not mean that one is better, more powerful or more special than the other. It is only a demonstration or expression that reveals where the mind has been focusing. Both are equal in their freedom and power of Love to choose. The power and principle of creation is afforded equally to both.

This world has played you on your need for specialness. That is your egoic consciousness incessantly seeking and striving. You need and seek such things as the car, the money, and the fame to feel special. This need for specialness emboldens you with a greater sense for comparison, contrast, criticism, competition, polarities, differences, fighting, approval, and survival. You consequently idolize athletes, celebrities, gurus, masters, heroes, mothers, fathers, money, fame, trophies, cars, possessions, et cetera.

You can see how strong the need is for specialness in all aspects of society —sports, entertainment, religion, countries, families, friends, homes, cars, phones, clothes, et cetera—. This is the nutting ego screaming, "I am separate from you. Look at me, look at me. Look how great I am." Meanwhile God is coolly saying, "No you nut. You are not separate from me. Look at all of me. Without me, you are nothing."

Daryl Chang

The need for specialness breeds judgment, comparison, competition, and violence. You get into a "you-versus-them" mindset and "winning is everything" philosophy to some degree with disregard for the well-being of your brothers and sisters.

Where is this need coming from? From outside of you. There is no freedom where there is need. Your need prevents you from doing what you truly desire, makes you do things you do not want to do, and gives you rationale or excuses to do harmful things.

You have been so engrained in need, your mind will say, "But I have all these things I have to do. What about this and what about that?" Will the world stop existing if you stop needing? That is up to the world, not up to you.

There is only God. God is pure unlimited eternal spirit. God has and is everything. You and God are one. God provides you everything. It is your natural inheritance. What need have you for money? What need have you to survive? What need have you of need? None.

The truest and wisest teachers of all are not from any man but from life elements such as the sun and all of nature. Through astute observation and contemplation, you can understand God and who you are.

You take the sun for granted. Each and every day, the sun radiates its light, energy, and warmth to all. It does not ask to be worshipped. It does not judge anything (ie. good or evil, right or wrong) and whether to give of itself or not. It does not ask for repayment in kind. It gives freely, unconditionally, and endlessly. It does not contemplate death. It does not perish. It existed when you were born and it will exist when you physically die. It does not cry, mourn, or stand still for you. It is oblivious to the things you deem good or evil, beautiful or ugly, right or wrong, et cetera. It is oblivious to war, poverty, dis-ease, and all other apparent atrocities. It is oblivious to your existence, what you do and what happens to you. No matter what you do, even if it "bad or evil", it never curses you, anyone or anything for that matter. It gives to you, the flower, the tree, the water, the air, the mountains, et cetera. It gives to the bad person, the good person, the ugly person, the beautiful person, the tyrant, the oppressed, et cetera. It is constant without judgment. It wants nothing from no one. It needs nothing from any one. It shows its magnificence and emanates its essence in spite of it all. It cannot and does not shine with specialness upon anyone at any time. It shines on all. The sun is what it is and does what it does —*Love and Love respectively*—. All it knows is to be.

All that can be said about the sun, you can say the same for the moon, air, water, flowers, trees, mountains, earth, and all of nature. They emit their glory independent of you, humanity, and the rest of nature. Man is God's greatest creation made in Its image and likeness. Unlike other creations, man has the capacity to reflect, to know, and to embody consciously that which is Love. God wonders, "These creations have a mind of their own. I give them Love to flow through their veins but they tie themselves in knots and it doesn't flow smoothly. They do not blossom fully like I intended."

Love pervades you and everyone else.

To love is let things be as they are in the sanctity of their own existence. To love is to always remember God is Love, that you are that same Love as you are created to be, that God is all in all, that you are one with all, and thus see yourself in another and another in yourself. To love is to see the content —Love—, not the form in another though they see it not within themselves but the pure unlimited spirit you both equally are, and thus extend the Love of itself. To love is to always remember that you are one with God and all, that all are One Mind, that their mind is touching yours and yours is touching theirs, and thus transmit Love. To love is to recognize the likes of criticism, anger, and guilt exhibited by another as fear within them, as a lack of recognition or forgetfulness of the Love within themselves, as one who is in fact suffering and crying for help and healing, and thus extend Love so that that one has the opportunity to remember and to get it. To love is to be like the sun shining, the wind blowing, or the river flowing, and extend Love without specialness to anyone or anything. To love is to remember you create it all, so to experience the likes of criticism, anger, or guilt is to recognize it as a creation of fear within yourself and an opportunity to heal yourself of that fear. To love another is an act to love yourself. To love is to know that fear is an illusion and that only Love is real.

Let us look at how this insane world affects one who is unawakened.

Everything (ie. cells, animals, insects, plants, people, places, et cetera) is pleomorphic. This means that things are not fixed entities but are able to assume different forms. They change from their original perfect

Daryl Chang

form to another perfect form according to their environment. That is, change the conditions and you change the form. Conditions influence how things exist and appear.

All things in their original natural state are perfect. They must be for it is in its self-interest to exist and to sustain its existence and perfection. Supreme Intelligence has and is the natural intelligence to be perfect. That is what It is and what It does. A thing deviates from its perfection when Supreme Intelligence is hindered, tampered with, or removed from It, whether consciously or unconsciously, intentional or not.

In health and science, there are two theories: (1) germ theory and (2) terrain theory. Germ theory, the one this false world operates on, blames the germ for the cause of illness. Terrain theory states that the germ is not the cause of illness but rather *appears* if at all because of the terrain (ie. environmental conditions). The terrain provides a reason or the means for its existence. The terrain influences the forms that take shape.

Cells are pleomorphic so as the environment becomes impure or corrupt, they morph into mutated cells that scientists proudly identify and label an illness. The germ which exists to perform a practical function may conveniently appear alongside the cells and prejudiced scientists conclude from its existence that it is the cause of said dis-ease.

Here is an example or analogy that may make clearer to you the germ/terrain theories and the principles of nature consistently operating. Let us say you drop a piece of sweet fruit, cookie, or cake on the floor. What potentially happens? There is a good chance that bugs such as ants and flies appear. Germs of some sort (identified as bacteria) will eventually appear to break down the waste. Let us say that you continue to scatter more food scraps all around not caring to clean up the mess. You are likely to attract not only ants, flies, and more bugs but possibly mice and rats.

You show no care. Instead, you sustain unhygienic, unsanitary, and unclean conditions and the germs now flourish in the dirty environment you have built. More ants, flies, mice, rats, raccoons, et cetera appear. The appearance of a problem becomes larger the longer you leave it to be. Would you blame the critters as being the cause of your frustration, pain, suffering, your so-called illness or problem? No. You were the cause of your problem. You inflicted yourself through your lack of self-care and self-Love of your personal environment and perfection.

The boogeymen do not appear by pure chance. The forms appear and come only because you have welcomed them. They remain because you continue to act in the way that affirms you would prefer they stay. Remember, you are cause and the world of form is effect.

The germs and all the critters did not cause your pollution; they simply appeared because of it. They will thrive and thus give the illusion they are the cause of the pollution that increases but this is false. You have been conditioned to look and blame things outside of yourself rather than accept self-responsibility. You are the cause of your problems. Things outside of you appear to perform their function, a nature of their existence to metabolize the impure and filthy creations. They prosper because the conditions allow it. This predicament is outside of you for you to witness. It is absurd to think that by killing the germs and the critters you rid yourself of the problem. In fact, when you do try to eliminate them particularly germs, being pleomorphic, they adjust the nature of themselves to survive the onslaught. You create "superbugs" that strengthen themselves through the adversity. You have created an endless battle. Show self-Love and self-care. Tidy up the area instead and the problem disappears. Their existence is no longer warranted.

When you are sick, the germ that may appear inside of you is not the cause of your sickness. You create the unhealthy terrain inside your body by frequently eating junk and processed foods, saturating it with harmful chemicals and unnatural substances; by persistently thinking negative thoughts; by habitually stressing yourself thereby causing an imbalance of hormones. All these things make your internal body more susceptible and vulnerable to so-called germs, viruses, and bacteria to thrive. They may thrive but they are not the cause of any claimed illness but an effect.

Cells are pleomorphic and so an impure terrain causes a perfect cell to mutate into a mutated or cancerous cell. They have deemed a cancerous cell as bad and accused it of killing you, and you have believed them. Your body is not suicidal. It is a form and an act of self-preservation, resulting from the lack of self-Love you have shown yourself. To try and eliminate cancerous cells as a means for treatment is ineffective, inefficient, and counter-productive. By doing so, you are yet again attacking yourself to rid a wrongly perceived problem thus harming yourself further.

This false world has created for you an illusion of causes and conditioned you to look outside yourself for resolution. You look to doctors and drugs to rectify a situation that is of your own doing. Just as in the previous example, it is absurd to think that by killing perceived bad germs or "cancer" cells, you cure yourself of your problem. They did not cause it and will eventually return because the conditions you are still subconsciously cultivating remain. If you keep your internal system pure and undefiled, you do not create problems and thus require no resolution. Cleanse your body and mind, and the form of sickness disappears.

Negative emotions are all masks of fear that are an indication and result of lack of self-care, self-worth, and ultimately self-Love. All forms of dis-ease are a culmination of this lack of self-Love that produces the ripe conditions for the dis-ease, unique to you, to result.

When you look at society, the same conditions principle applies. A filthy, destitute, and impoverished section of a city will attract thieves, gangs, and criminals because the conditions are ripe for their existence and sustenance. They are not necessarily the cause for the deprived conditions. "There are thieves, gangs, and criminals even in rich neighbourhoods," I can hear you say. Yes, that is true. It is all relative. From a universal perspective, conditions exist there as well. The world is a physical stage reflecting the purity of the terrain and its inhabitants.

Change the conditions of the city to either "good" or "bad" and the essence of the city will correspondingly change. The principle works the same.

Everything in your life follows the same principle. You deviate from your natural state of perfection thus create the appearance of your problems; you create the conditions for them to exist and grow. Whether it is poverty, sickness, negative people, abusive relationships, enemies, you create it all. These formed events appear because you create the conditions for it to exist and prosper. You are cause and the world of form is effect.

The question that an unawakened one may naturally ask is "How do I create this?" It is easy to understand this principle with the food example because it is physical, it is physically outside of you, and you can relate to it with your physical senses. This is your current habit and conditioning. Invisible variables within you such as your thoughts, feelings, and beliefs contribute to the creation likewise of your life conditions and subsequent experiences.

Understanding why things exist and appear leads to another aspect of significance, that of influence. Everything is connected because it is all one —*God*—. As such, every thing potentially affects or influences every other thing.

As mentioned, a thing in its original natural state is perfect. It must be for it is in its self-interest to exist and to sustain its existence and perfection. Perfect good conditions allow it to continue its perfect state of existence. It exists so it appears. In similar fashion, each thing beside is originally in a perfect good state. However, if a thing is surrounded by conditions that are not-good and unlike God, it will begin to deviate from its perfect self.

In the food example, the initial conditions were pure and clean allowing the existing things to remain as they were. The prevalent conditions influence the state and evolution of the things that exist in those conditions. The new unclean conditions caused germs, ants, flies, mice, rats, et cetera to appear. As the impure conditions continue becoming the dominant state, they greatly influence the development and sustenance of not only those things that were existing prior but the newly introduced things that consequently appear.

In the example of your own body, the initial conditions were pure and clean allowing the existing cells to remain as they were. As time goes on, your internal system becomes polluted by the toxic environment (ie. pesticides, synthetics, household chemicals, et cetera) and by your own harmful behaviour (ie. eating processed foods with artificial flavours and colourings, drinking alcohol, smoking, allowing negative thoughts, stressing, et cetera). You are creating and sustaining impure conditions inside your body. As more cells become tainted thereby establishing impure conditions that become the dominant state, they greatly influence the development of the existing pure cells. As such, when cells becomes cancerous, they can run amuck creating cells like unto itself.

In an example of a city slum, there is an initial time when conditions were pure and clean. As time goes on, the thieves, gangsters, and criminals influence the inhabitants particularly pure and innocent children to become thieves, gangsters, and criminals themselves. Instead of being creators of a good life, they act as victims and allow the outside influence to dictate their behaviour. The unawakened good are more susceptible then to the influence of their bad environment.

Remind yourself that "need" is an expression of the perception that there is something you lack. This world is governing your beliefs that you need to be a certain way, that you need to be acceptable to others, that you need to conform and fit in, that you need to make money, and that you need to survive.

In not knowing the Truth of who you are, you have allowed this outside world to influence your being. You think fearful thoughts. You act in anger, frustration, and worry as those around you. You feel the need to be a certain way, to be acceptable to others, to conform and fit in, to make money, and to survive so you do as others do.

The insane world appears and remains because you are continually contributing to the impure conditions for its existence. The tyrants, murderers, and swindlers are the germ formations, metaphorically speaking, that appear because of them. Your fearful thoughts have helped create the ripe conditions. Extend only loving thoughts through the Mind of God instead and the insane world of bad actors will eventually disappear. They are you and you are them.

This world is based on the perception that conditions must be met before there can be a choice for peace instead of war, for forgiveness instead of judgment, for Love instead of fear. Hence, you think, "When the conditions outside of me change, then I will make the choice for peace, forgiveness, or Love."

This world is the reflection of the insane choice to deny Love and be devoted to fear instead. A complete reversal of thought is required to transform yourself and the world. This is why it is central to accept full personal responsibility and not to absolve yourself of it to a person, a company, a government, or anything outside of you. Your Love is dependent on you extending it from yourself. The dissolution of fear, war, and all negative things are dependent on you extending the Love that you are to the world.

Love is a grand thing. Love does not require any set of conditions to exist before It does.

Listen carefully. No one has the power to create your experience. Know that what others choose does not influence your choice. It begins when you assume full responsibility for your choices.

Let us take a moment to bring awareness to the repercussions on how you identify yourself.

You are pure unlimited spirit but when you know not the Truth, you do not identify with this. Instead, you identify with the body-mind. You identify with the perceptions of form through your physical senses, whether it be the body, a belief, a career, or a context of experience of any kind. You see a world of objects separated by space. You see across from you the body of a brother or sister and conclude that he or she is separate from you. You fail to see the subtle interconnection of all things, people, and events and the Love that permeates throughout. You forget that you live in the universe that is one thing containing many expressions.

You identify as a Canadian, an American, or a European, as a Catholic, a Buddhist, or a Muslim, as a fan of a sports team, as a coffee lover, and on and on it goes. You create identifications with small aspects of life and begin to take on beliefs, principles, and perceptions based upon whatever it is you identify with. Your mind interprets events and draws conclusions and then bases behaviour upon it. So from your unlimited self, you keep creating limits and limits and more limits, hence making yourself smaller and smaller and smaller and smaller. You are unwittingly using the power of God to create smallness, weakness, separation, and loneliness.

Through identification, you not only limit yourself but you limit others as well. You identify your brothers and sisters with similar identity boxes. Instead of seeing pure unlimited spirits of Love, you see limited loveless bodies with faults and imperfections. With each identity you perceive, you limit and limit and limit them. They appear to you smaller and smaller and smaller as you do with yourself.

Through the ego, you identify with the limiting definitions you have created of yourself. You identify with a name, a role, a title, a class, a job, a religion, a country, et cetera; something of form in the world.

You have placed boundaries on the box you see and live in. You judge and compare yourself with others strictly from form not recognizing it is just an experience you have chosen from your unlimited Self whether it result from fear or Love. In a sea of unawakened ones, you witness the world focused on form and differences, not the shared content — Love— and similarities.

When you identify yourself with the limiting definitions you self-create, you set yourself up for judgment. You will not be able to avoid judging your brother or sister who is not what you identify with. You will feel an air of specialness or superiority. You will consequently create separation. You will lose the presence of Love.

For instance, if you identify yourself as a vegetarian, you will judge another who is not. When you know the Truth of who you are, you are not influenced by anyone else's choices and their choices do not say anything about your own. You recognize that they are not doing something wrong and that their decision means nothing. It is just a description of how they are structuring their experience as you are. You are free to embrace your experience as they freely are too. You are free to extend Love nevertheless. As Love, you set things free.

When you give up your self-definitions and see the web of relationships with everything, you will gain more awe of God's Love in everything. You will see not the form in everything but the content —Love—. You have identified with the workings and fruit of this world for so long that you have identified with fear only and not your true nature and identity —Love—.

The egoic consciousness represented by the body-mind has the fear of death and survival and thus binds you to the world of form. It is this illusion of fear and identification with temporal form that takes you away from being the eternal Love that you truly are.

Understand well that what you identify with greatly influences how you see things and the way you live. They can hinder or help your progress to Love's presence.

In this present world, you perceive you are separate from God; you perceive that what you see in physical form is reality; you perceive that you are not entirely in control but at times a victim of circumstances; you perceive that you are the body-mind bounded by all forms; you perceive limitations and that not all things are possible; you admit that feeling fear feels not-good but you perceive that it is natural; you perceive that a government authority must exist to govern you; you perceive you lack things. These perceptions or things that you identify with hinder your progress to Love's presence.

Explore what happens when you shift your identity. That is, you are one with God; you recognize that what you see in physical form is all an illusion that arises and passes away over time; you are in complete control and never a victim of circumstances because you recognize that you are a creator of everything; you are the Power using the power to create everything; you are pure unlimited spirit unbounded by any form; you are limitless and nothing is impossible; you admit that feeling Love feels good and that it is your natural state of being; you are your own authority and need no other outside of you to govern you; you recognize that you have been given everything so you have no need of need. Identifying with these things helps your progress to Love's presence. Thus, identify with God who is only Love. Let this be the reality that blossoms and allow everything else to crumble. When you shift your perspective, know and live Truth, you will advance in the path to Love.

Everything you do is a habit —a subconscious pattern you repeat—. You are what you repeatedly do.

A habit becomes a habit when you subconsciously do it without your conscious recognition of it. It is not inherently a good or bad, right or wrong thing. It is simply the nature of how you operate in your existence. Riding a bicycle, driving a car, playing a guitar, et cetera are all habits you master without having to consciously relearn the task every moment. It is an automated operation integrated into your being that results because of your intentional focus.

In like fashion, when you focus on anything, whether consciously or not, the habit will become integrated into your being. Focus on fear often and you will automatically operate on fear as your natural state, which it is not. Conversely, focus on Love often and you will automatically operate on Love as your natural state, which it is.

Everything is a habit or an addiction, even things you may perceive in another context such as an attribute, state, or dimension. That is, Love, fear, thought, avarice, envy, gluttony, sloth, judgment, criticism, joy, poverty, sickness, et cetera are all habits.

This false world filled with falsities and ruled by a false god has made you develop false addictions. When you expand the consciousness of who you are, you will realize that all these outside attachments or addictions are temporary and unfulfilling. Everything that you need to achieve a permanent sense of balance is within you.

They of this false world ruled by a false god know you are ignorant of your divinity and do everything to sustain your lack of consciousness of your divinity. They resourcefully create and build the thoughts and habits they wish you to have so that you create, build, and sustain the false world of form they benefit from.

This false world intentionally keeps you overwhelmed, busy, stressed, and confused; creates a relentless noisy and distracting environment; engenders fear and anxiety to keep you in survival mode; makes you feel exhausted and defeated; exploits animals, people, and nature to desensitize you so you accept it as normal; poisons you through the air, water, and food with chemicals, pesticides, and synthetic products in pretence of human safety; indoctrinates you through churches, schools, and society with teachings that advance its agenda.

You are an addict. You are addicted to this false world and all its false shenanigans. You are like the cocaine addict who is so deep into the addiction, you beg and need your constant shot of cocaine to sustain your existence or you feel you will succumb to your death. The dealer benefits from your addiction and so accommodates it. He gives you more cocaine in the form of wars, poverty, dis-ease, tyranny, disasters, violence, oppression, famine, drugs, alcohol, pollution, pornography, animal cruelty, planet destruction, massacres, genocide, pedophilia, human trafficking, et cetera by breeding more fear, anger, hatred, competition, frustration, hopelessness, stress, anxiety, depression, et cetera into you. He administers the cocaine not through a needle but via television, movies, music, social media, sports, video games, politicians, churches, schools, et cetera. You no longer question your suffering but instead relish your dark drama, a perverse addiction.

Smoking, alcohol, drugs, coffee, sugar, salt, violence, sex, money, lies, power, vanity, et cetera are all admittedly pleasurable addictions to satisfy physical lust. Even food which you perceive as necessary for physical survival is similarly an addiction. They do not serve spiritual fulfillment but rather are used as a means to elevate your state of mind. You perceive you do these activities because you want to for social, entertainment, pleasure, or amusement purposes but they are primarily a means to escape pain, thought, or the ungodly life you deem normal. You are out of control.

When you are addicted, "good", "bad", "harmful", and "damaging" are irrelevant concepts. When you, the addicted individual, is in an intolerable state of mind, you focus only on the short-term benefit of achieving a temporary state of gratification and relief that comes from the means you use to get there. You do not think nor care about the costs and consequences of your addictions. The drawbacks to the quality of your life (ie. health, relationships, finances, happiness, et cetera) in general are of secondary concern.

You think that your addiction is to that "thing" but it is not. Your addiction is to the state of mind that the experience of the "thing" provides. You are continually wanting to attain a sense of balance; a state of mind of lasting peace, clarity, and well-being. Your addiction is an illusion which you falsely believe will help you find lasting balance. Ironically, it serves only to send you deeper into the addiction and further out of balance. You are endlessly trying to fill a hole in yourself, something that is missing. That something is Love, self-Love.

You are ultimately addicted to fear. All negative addictions derive from this primary addiction. Fear is the illusion of power and the energy source of the false god. Fear is a learned unnatural state. When you live so long in hatred and fear of your fellow human beings, you greatly develop your faculty of hatred and fear. That is all you know and who you become. You separate yourself completely from God, your divinity, hence your brothers and sisters. It is evident that there are varying degrees of separation in this world —some are extremely separated, some are modestly separated, some are marginally separated—. All are nonetheless unaware of their divinity and thus become more separated to some degree each moment.

The moment you realize who you are —*God*— and that you create it all, you will realize that you can change it all. With the realization you create everything comes the realization that you can create anything you want. You create anything you want by aligning yourself with God and thinking with the Mind of God.

Daryl Chang

The moment you realize who you are —*God*— and that you are Love, you will realize you have no "addictions" but natural tendencies which equate to you being in your natural state. In accepting your divinity, you have self-Love, self-acceptance, self-worth, self-confidence, self-belief, et cetera. Your apparently new habits are still pleasurable and personally satisfying but you no longer shift back to a negative state of mind. You achieve the permanent state of balance where there is lasting peace, clarity, and contentment.

We make a declaration here that may seem obvious now.

— You are in a bad dream. —

Would you intentionally dream a bad dream, a nightmare? The answer is, "No, you would not." You dream a bad dream when you are unconscious, you are sleeping, you are dreaming. A bad dream comes about because you believe the forms you see and experience are real. But the forms are illusions borne from the mind of fear. You come out of the bad dream when you awaken, when you come back to your senses, when you become conscious again. And this is what you are doing right here, right now. You are awakening. Awakening means remembrance. You remember who you are and where you are. You are Love caught up in fear, a bad dream, and you are now coming back to reality. When you awaken from a bad dream, you feel a sense of relief and peace knowing that it was just a dream. When you awaken, you then consciously, deliberately, and authentically live as you truly desire.

This bad dream which appeared permanent is but a temporary illusion. To resist illusion is to insist that the illusion is real. The cause of your resistance is fear. Fear prevents the acceptance of Truth thus denies the Love you seek and inhibits reality from emerging. Do not deny it. Do not agonize over this realization any longer. Know it. Accept it for what it is and was. Embrace it. Love it. Move on. Get on with your G(o)od self.

It takes vigilance and discipline to always remember each day not to fall asleep again. This is the great temptation, tendency, irony, tragedy, and comedy of this world. To repeatedly think that all those around you, walking in their sleep, are more knowledgeable, more intelligent, wiser, and better than you. It seems like everybody is sleepwalking and doing what they do so it must be right and you must do as they do. Phooey! Utter nonsense.

You have allowed others to hijack your mind and thoughts. Put another way, you have not originated your own thoughts; instead you have lazily taken the thoughts and beliefs of others and the world as your own. You are not behaving sovereignly and thinking independently for yourself. You are in fear of social exclusion and so you have "sold your soul" in exchange for the perception of social acceptance. You have repressed your own individual creative thought to autonomously direct your own life as you desire.

Insanity seems sane to those insane. That is just the way it is. When many dodo birds are walking off the cliff to their own detriment, will you dimly choose to follow along and do the same? You can choose to be different —real, sane, Love—. Be a crazy one in this world who assumes responsibility, accepts Truth, and commits to listening to no other voice than that of God —Love—. You, the awakened one, may not be understood, approved of, or acknowledged by others of this false world. How can the insane understand the sane? Those who are sleeping need someone to stir them from their slumber. You are now such someone.

The Truth is simple. You will awaken from the dream of this insane world when you hold steadily within the mind: "Only Love is real. You are not the body but pure unlimited spirit. You and God are one. You are only Love. You are God in a unique form walking this Earth. You choose Love over fear under all circumstances, always. You are free as you are created to be."

Freedom is Love under all conditions.

Love makes you see the good, the light,
the perfection, and the spirit of all things.

PART
THREE

The Reality

♦

THREE

Now what?

After every accomplishment, achievement, or attainment, is it not generally true you ask, "Now what?" You have the money, the car, the house, the marriage, the kids, now what? You achieved fame, now what? You achieved success, whatever that is to you, now what? You sang the song, wrote the book, painted the masterpiece, now what?

You had some idea that at the end of doing this, getting that, achieving this or accomplishing that, that you would be "happy", "at peace", "fulfilled" but for some reason, you still feel you are not. You have this nagging thought, "There must be more than this."

You ask, "Now what?" because you deeply know there is more to it than the stuff this insane world makes you believe are important. You successfully kept yourself distracted or found ways to avoid the fundamental gnawing questions of "Who am I?" and "What is my purpose?" A true understanding is the answer of all answers.

You learn of your divinity, now what?

I have painted several masterpieces, read a few books and written a few books, planted a garden, built a deck, baked cakes, cooked delicious meals, taught classes, hiked mountains, played many a sport, made love, helped friends and strangers, danced the night away, and so much more. There is one common truth in all —Love—. I loved doing it. I loved creating things. I loved playing. I loved working with my mind and hands. I loved sharing what I love with others. I loved helping others. I loved teaching, empowering, and inspiring others. I loved witnessing and being in nature. I loved being appreciated. I loved seeing others appreciate. I loved seeing others in Love, joy, and happiness. I loved seeing others do whatever it is they love doing. I love the feeling of Love. I love witnessing any and all acts of Love. I love all things God.

It was not about acquiring great power. It was not about achieving fame. It was not about attaining vast wealth. It was not about helping you or about you. It was not necessarily about accomplishing anything grand in particular. It was not about achieving some grand mystical state of consciousness. It was just about being Love, extending Love, and experiencing Love. It brought me joy.

There was never a "Now what?" It was more like "What next?" The fact that I always have a next moment can only mean that something else is living me.

Learning of my divinity awakened me to who I am and what this means. It made me conscious of creating consciously instead of what I was doing unconsciously. I innately knew things I did not know why I knew. When I had a thought, which was that still small voice speaking to me, I did not think much of it. I would think it, feel like doing it, and went about doing it. In doing such things, I would not notice time flying by.

When I was seeking the Truth, I had no idea what I was actually pursuing. I did not know why or what it meant. I just had this unwavering desire to seek this something. It was like looking with intention for anything such as that home, girl, or shirt and someone asks, "What are you looking for?" You do not really know what it is till you come across it. You know it when you find it.

My persistent seeking of the Truth is no more for what I seek, I have found. It is the realization and awareness that what I seek is within me. I am the Truth. I am the Truth that sets my Self free. I am the Power of God. To know God, I must be God. If I am to know the Love of God, I must be Love only under all conditions. I am the Love that heals my Self. I am my own problem and my own solution.

I have allowed this insane world to taint me and my heart, and pervert who I am. Now that I remember who I am, I recognize that I do not need to fix anything, anyone, or the world. There was nothing and there is nothing to fix. If I think with the mind unlike God, and think that there is something wrong with the world that needs fixing, then I will cause the universe to bestow upon me a world of wrongness that needs fixing. If I think that the universe is unfriendly and does not support me, then I will experience a world that proves to me such a thought is true. This compulsion, this need to get involved, this need to fix is baseless for again it comes from a perception. The world is nothing more than my own mental creation. I choose to see only God —Love— and thus reveal to me that God is Truth.

My only function is to be the presence of Love; to love; to extend the treasure of my very Self. There is nothing to do but just be —Love—. I just am. I am Love so I am free. I am free because I am Love. To be free always, I must be Love under all conditions. I set myself free. I set all things and others free.

I no longer look to see how I can make things different or better than they are. I look only, and live from, what I most truly desire; to abide in my own nature that is Love and to allow Life to flow from that nature, in the infinite myriad displays of form.

May you embrace your divinity and no longer seek Love, joy, peace, happiness, or anything because you recognize now that it is within you, that it *is* you. You no longer think "Now what?" because you experience fulfillment in each moment being the Love you are just because. You are in perpetual joy of being and creating. You are in the flow of eternal nows. You and God are one. There is nothing you have to do to get God because you already are. There are only some things that you need to release or remove such as beliefs, judgments, perceptions, and projections so that God can get you. Everything is to support you for a happy existence. You are free to live in the highest joy, to ask for what you want, and to open the heart and love.

In fact, it may even be simpler than that. You recognize you have a bad habit and so you just replace it with a newer better habit. You have been judging, perceiving, and projecting. When you think about it, this is a lot of work that just creates more work, pain, and suffering. It is exhausting. Stopping this work means less work or no work and more time to play. Allow only thoughts from the Mind of God into your consciousness. That is, have loving thoughts only and act on them when asked within. And bless every creation that comes into your awareness. That is your lone task. How much simpler can it be?

When you grasp the simplicity of this, you will better appreciate how it actually requires less effort. The beauty is in the effortlessness. You will be like the blade of grass that exerts no effort to grow; the sun that exerts no effort to shine; or the wind that exerts no effort to blow. You will simply sway from the Life of Love that flows through you.

Daryl Chang

Learn to observe what you are really doing every moment even in the most pedestrian things. For instance, when you drop by the coffee shop, receive your cup of coffee, look into the eye of the person who gives it to you, smile and say, "Thank you," you have succeeded in extending Love. You have acted in Truth. You have remembered who you are and that the one in front of you is worthy of your respect and Love. You do this all the time except when you do not. This insane world entraps and conditions you to unnaturally withhold Love through methods of fear. Each time you can interrupt the momentum of the misperceptions of this world, you will know the undercurrent of Love is within you still. Little by little, you will cultivate the power necessary to be identified with only that One Mind.

When I reflect on my present conditions, I recognize that if I lack something, have not accomplished something I desire, or experience something I do not want, it is because to some degree, I am operating and focused on hidden fears; lack of self-worthiness; what I do not want; what is not possible; the worst outcome; inaction; judgment; attachment; resistance. I am afraid, pessimistic, and unenthusiastic of being "lesser" than where I am. This is *not* the God within me who is unlimited, eternal, and infinite wanting to expand myself. I recognize that I am of egoic consciousness when I feel any hint of fear. Fear miscreates.

When I reflect on my present conditions, I recognize that if I have something or have accomplished something I desire, it is because I am operating and focused on Love; self-worthiness; what I do want; what is possible; the best outcome; action; non-judgment; non-attachment; non-resistance. I am bold, optimistic, and enthusiastic of being "more" than where I am. This is the God within me who is unlimited, eternal, and infinite wanting to expand myself. I recognize that I am of God consciousness when I feel propelled by Love. Love creates.

Imagine for a moment, someone who is the most incompetent, incapable, or incapacitated human being yet she is the most loving, kind, and compassionate in the world. How do you think this individual would fare or "survive" in this current world? Do you think their existence has any value? Imagine if this person is you?

Now imagine someone who is the most competent, capable, or skilled human being yet he is the most hateful, cruel, and callous in the world.

Suspend your beliefs temporarily. Withdraw your attachment to all of the things this world has conditioned you to attach with value. Simplify the nature of your own consciousness.

Which of the two aforementioned individuals would you prefer to be? If you were to meet the two individuals, who would you rather spend time or be with? Reflect on your answers. Did they come quickly to you? Were your responses influenced by the way you perceive the world is or by the way the world you wish it to be?

A part of you innately knew an immediate answer to these questions yet you may have possibly hesitated and suppressed it. If this is so, ask yourself why. I am guessing that you kind of wanted to be neither and both. That is, not the most incompetent, incapable, or incapacitated in the world and not the most hateful, cruel, and callous one; but the most loving, kind, and compassionate in the world and the most competent, capable, or skilled as well.

There is another subtle element beyond projection as to why you are triggered when someone acts unlike God. When someone is rude to you, you are angered because you intrinsically recognize that that person is not being the Love as they should be. They are unconscious of who and what they are. You innately want to extend Love because that is what you are but they are making it a challenge. They are actually crying out for help and healing but you do not recognize this, even of yourself. Therein lies the irony and comedy. If you do not know who or what you are either, you act as they do and reciprocate the rude behaviour. You contribute to the sustenance of poor habits. You resist or refrain from extending your Love. You give the other power to affect you and divert you from being who you are. You act as if you seek something from the other and as if you lack or need it. It is a circle of insanity. It is the dog chasing its own tail. It is the hamster running on the wheel thinking it is getting somewhere.

For the chance of ending the insanity, someone has to choose or decide to extend Love without attachment. Someone has to want nothing, seek nothing, and be merely the presence of Love. Someone has to first awaken to their true Self and accept full responsibility. One who is unawakened does not actually prevent you, who are awakened, from being who you are.

Daryl Chang

If you do not bring forth what is within you —Love—, what is within you will destroy you. If you bring forth what is within you —Love—, what is within you will save you.

Anyone can be joyful and loving in a candy store. Anyone can be loving with strangers if they are applauding you. Anyone can be loving with friends and family who say they love you. But only the awakened can be loving when those strangers, friends, and family have chosen to crucify you.

This Life on Earth you perceive is a game of consciousness, where the environment and challenges continuously adjust according to the mastery of your innate Power and Love. You are playing a 'hide-and-seek' game whereby you are God seeking God for the enjoyment of finding and knowing God again. You are to heal your sense of separation from God. You are here to learn of Love and to live in the Truth of who you are.

This game has no regulation stop time and no final level. It is unlike any game you have come to know and play. It is eternal and has no practical ending except possibly from the death of the body that is used as a temporary communication game device in the world of form. It is not about winning or losing anything. It is not about survival. It is about growth and expansion of Love. It is about playing for the sheer joy of it and enjoying the experience, as typical with all games.

When you view Life or existence as a game you choose to play rather than as something you have to do or get through, you anticipate ups and downs. You eventually come to see the beauty of the game and enjoy the game when you get on top of it, when you begin to master it.

If you prefer, you can view this plane as a school. Every moment is a teaching moment for you to learn about yourself and Love. Every experience is a unique test and a stepping stone toward the ultimate achievement, perfect union with God —your atonement, your at-one-ment. The curriculum is for you to master your innate Power and Love.

When you view Life or existence as a school you choose to go to rather than as something you have to do or get through, you welcome the tests so that you can gauge how you are progressing. You enjoy the journey of getting better just as you would with playing a guitar, playing tennis, or what-have-you. You gain satisfaction and fulfilment from your accomplishments amidst frustrations during the learning process. You are continually delighted, recognizing how far you have come from where you started.

All the things and people of this insane world love to keep pulling you down and keeping you from the Truth, the beauty and worthiness of who you truly are. But you are like a humble and disciplined artist or athlete who cultivates and refines the skill wanting to extend your treasure, that greater beauty into the world out of sheer delight.

Perhaps you have reverted to thinking, "This all sounds nice and I do like all this stuff about God and Love but I have all these things I have to get done. I am a good person. I am not someone going around killing people. What about all these other people who are being harmful?"

How is it possible to see your brother or sister as God sees his children, especially when your brother or sister is harmful? To see with the eyes of God begins with the acceptance that you, as a creator —created in the image of God— literally choose every experience and call it to yourself, that you create the veils through which you view creation. That is, you acknowledge that you are a creator always and you accept complete responsibility for all that you see and experience because you recognize that you are the one —God— who is creating it all, no one else. Everything that comes to you is because you have called it from within yourself in order to grow more deeply in forgiveness, in wisdom, in Love, and in the Mind of God. There is only God, showing up as you.

When someone acts badly or wrongly in this world (ie. unlike God) especially if it is against or toward you, look upon them as one who does not know how to live in this world without being of this world, who does not know the way to self-forgiveness, who does not know the Truth of the Love that lives within them, and who does not recognize their great power to create whatever they want in a way that is not harmful to anyone.

Recognize that one who acts in anger, hatred, envy, sadness, et cetera is actually one who is suffering inside and is crying out for help and healing though they themselves know not. Rather than react to them in a reciprocating manner, look upon them with compassion. By teaching Love, you open a window of opportunity for that one to recognize it in themself and you give them permission to do the same too.

Daryl Chang

Start from a place of understanding, compassion, acceptance, and ultimately unconditional Love. Offering Love is not condoning the behaviour that is unlike God. It is simply offering understanding that you cannot fully know the depth of the pain and suffering of mind they are experiencing. Know that your resistance to an afflicted individual's behaviour is part of the energy that only furthers the person to confirm his or her lack of self-worth.

As one who has awakened, you are always conscious that you and God are one, that all things are simply one thing appearing in different forms —cars, plants, trees, sun, clouds, animals, your brothers and sisters, thoughts arising and passing away—. They are but one thing. You are singular and you are every thing.

You begin to move away from striving for God, striving for perfection, striving to be good, striving to fix people, striving to fix the world, and begin to cultivate within yourself the process of allowing. You choose to surrender every perception you conjure up about your brother or sister that would veil the Truth —Love— that is true about them always. When one is hating, berating, or lambasting you, you will not respond with defensiveness but with curiosity and innocence. You choose to not taint the Truth with your own perceptions, judgments, feelings, and behaviour. You choose to persistently forgive which is also an act of forgiving yourself. You choose to embrace things with innocence.

The more you practice the aforementioned, the veils will dissolve from the mind and the more Love will shine forth. When you exhibit Love in the midst of another crucifying you, you will confess that you feel good. Conversely, when you exhibit fear or deny Love in the likes of anger, impatience, and frustration, you will admit that you feel not-good. When you truly reflect, you will observe that you feel much better about yourself when exhibiting Love compared to when you habitually react in fear, anger, or impatience and lash out another.

Know that anger, hatred, envy, negative behaviour and actions are never justified. They are all founded upon fear. Those that behave negatively and unlike God are crying out in their own fear and insanity. Remember like begets like. If one wrongs you and you spend energy convincing them they have wronged you, you call to yourself the energy likes of fear, conflict, judgment, unhappiness, and separation instantly. But if you forgive, you call instead the energy likes of unconditional Love, peace, and atonement. When you are wronged, understand you have power. All such opportunities merely provide you the opportunity to choose the Power of Love. Do not allow yourself to get pulled into the drama. Honour the Truth and who you are. Transcend the insanity of this world.

You are not angry, sad, anxious, or any negative emotion for the reasons you think. Yes, your dog died, your partner left you, or you got swindled. Yet the essence and power of Love has not left you for you are still free to Love and create as you desire. You are sad, angry, or anxious because the experience is senseless and foolish. The experience is senseless and foolish because you are God and it is not of God's Kingdom. You are God and this does not make any sense at all hence your negative reaction. It is meaningless. It is meaningless because it is a meaningless world. It is an insane world. But you are unawakened to the Truth of who you are so you are confused. Your negative emotion, pain, and suffering are a result of this confusion.

This does not mean that you cannot and will not get sad, angry, or anxious yourself. It also does not mean you should judge or condemn yourself when you yourself do for that is judgment itself. It means you recognize it for what it is and correct it.

When you operate on Love, you focus on what you desire without any attachment to them. The answers come into your reality based on who you are because God is anxious to give it to you as you are to get it. Your role is to know you are worthy, see and claim it. When you love yourself, you love God; when you love God, you love not only yourself, but everyone and everything.

There is an eternal state of realities coinciding with yours. Each person, place, or thing is God expressing the perfection of matching intents, and providing a learning opportunity of Love for all involved. It is an eternal dance and play of creation. God is always working with elegant precision, unfaltering intelligence, and deep wisdom.

You have a greater impact on people by who you are rather than by what you have or what you do.

The most effective way to help in the healing of another human being is to be the God that you inherently are. When you are, you come from a place of understanding, compassion, acceptance, and unconditional

Love. This is because you are the Love that you are —*God*—. When you are not at this level of understanding and being (ie. you judge, criticize, condemn, refute, resist an afflicted individual's behaviour, et cetera), you affirm a person's lack of self-worth. The more you know God loves and accepts you, the more you can offer this Love and acceptance to yourself and others. You let your own light shine so that you unconsciously give others permission to do the same. When they see and experience the God in you, they will begin to see it in themselves. They will come closer to knowing God is within them too.

We are all One Mind. Each person who knows of their divinity and accepts it contributes to helping those unaware become aware. *You are now one such person.* The greatest treasures in Heaven —your home— are you and the people you help to get there. Raise yourself and you will raise others.

It feels good when you hug someone or someone hugs you. You feel the warmth, beauty, and safety in your heart from the embrace. The physical act displays the union of two apparent separate parts. In like fashion, God is pressing upon your Being all around, everywhere in every moment. Recognize the same principle and feeling of Love demonstrated by the spiritual arms of God embracing you. God abides in you and you abide in God.

No matter what anybody else is doing, embody only the reality of Love. Do not tolerate judgment in yourself —of anyone or anything—. Forgive everyone and everything. Never compare your experience with another person. Yours is unique. Bring awareness to each moment and allow it to teach you how to forgive, how to trust, how to embrace, how to allow, how to love and therefore how to live fully. You are a child of God and you are here in this world to bring Light to it and to express the infinite nature of Love and creativity.

Creativity is always expressing itself out of energy. Love and fear are both energies. In this insane world where you do not know of Truth, your creativity is expressed out of fear, not out of pure Love and joy as it rightly should be. It is like an awakened aficionado who takes a flute and plays a melodious tune, while an unawakened hack takes the same flute and plays cacophony. Both produce sound but of different quality.

You are definitively eternal unlimited power and freedom for creativity. You are ceaselessly creating based on the energy you choose to use.

Awaken to the Truth, shift to pure Love energy and you create blessed creations.

As you assimilate more the Love that you are, you will see the quality of forms that come into your life change. Yet you will not be attached to them for you will not see them as ends in themselves but merely as proof of the great wisdom of Love.

Choose to not be deceived by this world any longer. Choose to not be a doormat for other people's perceptions. Choose to know the Truth of who you are, to follow your own path, and to never again be a pawn of any government, group, faction, or anyone. Choose to live the Truth of who you are.

You are the one with power, dominion, and choice over your own existence. You are free to choose only loving thoughts or only fearful thoughts. But it is you who must accept responsibility for your choices and not abdicate it to someone else such as an employer, a government, a friend, a family member, or whoever and then conveniently blame the result of your choices on that other. Claim your divinity. Exercise your power rightly.

Learning the Truth and learning to forgive are the ways to heal and free your Self. There is no more seeking, no more "Now what?"

Deep in our hearts, is Love not what we all want and yearn for? Is Love not what we all want to give of ourselves? Do we not wish that someone loves us unconditionally and magnificently? Every soul longs to know Love. You just want to love and be loved. At this point, may you know that what you want and yearn for is already within you, that what you want to give you can because it is within you, that someone – God– does love you unconditionally and grandly. That is, you are loved, you are loving, and you are forever lovable. Your fulfillment does not exist in gaining Love from another but in giving Love to everyone.

Take a moment to reaffirm the commitment you made at the start. When you have read the words you have read and it resonates within you as the Truth, know it to be so. If this Truth did not already live within you as the reality of your existence, you would not recognize it otherwise. You are remembering that part of you that is Love itself.

Your transfiguration is in progress. Allow and embrace it. You have no more interest in serving or defending the ego. You are no longer concerned about seeking Heaven on Earth. You are not even concerned about bringing Heaven on Earth to this world though it may result. You are only interested in abiding in your own true nature and allowing the Life of Love to flow from that nature. You are well on your way.

Do not delay. Do now waste time any longer. Decide firmly on what you will hold with the greatest value. When you judge another, you are proclaiming that you value fear, conflict, and your separation from God. When you practice forgiveness, you are proclaiming that you value Love, peace, and your union with God. So, value and commit to Love and God only not to fear and that unlike God.

Cultivate the Mind of God of wholly loving thoughts only. There are only two options —Love or fear, reality or illusion, Truth or falsity, sanity or insanity, peace or conflict, joy or suffering, unlimitedness or smallness, atonement or separation, awakening or sleep, resurrection or crucifixion, forgiveness or judgment, creator or victim, God or ego—. Every moment is pure and innocent and you are eternally free to choose. Choose consciously and deliberately.

Your transfiguration rests simply on your decision to accept the Truth that is true always and to live Truth in every moment; your willingness to take God at God's word.

There is only God. All is God. God is but perfect Love. You and God are one. It is not possible for God to be separate from Itself. You are as God created you to be. You are perfect Love as well. You allow all things, embrace all things, trust all things, and thereby transcend all things. You set all things free. You set yourself free.

You are what you long for. You are It. You are the One who becomes what you perceive as the many yet remains always the One —God—. Only Love is real. All else is illusion. What is real cannot be threatened by what does not truly exist. Love is eternal; it is never lost. You are not the body. Your body only serves you as a conduit or vessel to express Love. You need do nothing but let the Life of Love flow through you. You are here to extend Love and bless with gratitude all of creation. You are here to lovingly create as you desire that which extends the treasure that is you; to create unique expressions of the Love within you.

Freedom is Love under all conditions. When you are perfect Love, then you are perfectly free. You are perfectly free, always. You are perfectly free to extend Love. You are Power and you are free to choose what you want to perceive and to elicit what you want to feel, always. Choose Love over fear under all circumstances, always. Love is all there is. This is the reality. Own it. Honour yourself. Come back home.

Daryl Chang

Always follow your heart.

The heart is that which guides you to what you truly desire, brings you most joy, and streams your innate Love.

Your heart is that which feels all things, embraces all things, trusts all things, allows all things and thereby transcends all things.

LOVE

IS WHO YOU ARE

*get out of the way and
let Love live through you*

ONLY LOVE
IS REAL

www.ingramcontent.com/pod-product-compliance
Lightning Source LLC
Chambersburg PA
CBHW052125090426
42741CB00009B/1962